In the Days of Paul

Anthony J. Tambasco

In the Days of Paul

The Social World and Teaching
of the Apostle

Wipf & Stock
PUBLISHERS
Eugene, Oregon

Wipf and Stock Publishers
199 W 8th Ave, Suite 3
Eugene, OR 97401

In The Days of Paul
The Social World and Teaching of the Apostle
By Tambasco, Anthony J.
Copyright©1991 Paulist Press
ISBN: 1-59752-836-6
Publication date 7/25/2006
Previously published by Paulist Press, 1991

This limited edition licensed by special permission of Paulist Press.
www.paulistpress.com

Contents

Introduction 1

The World of Paul 13

Beginnings of the Mission 29

Thessalonians and Philippians 45

The Church in Corinth 61

Continued Corinthian Correspondence 76

The Church in Galatia 89

Roman Christianity 101

Appendix: Colossians and Ephesians 113

Suggestions for Additional Reading 124

*Dedicated with affection to
Rod, Adeline and Pat
and to the memory of
Adeline*

Introduction

If there is, after Jesus, any person of stature and importance in the early church, that person is Paul. Yet the second letter of Peter in the New Testament itself, tells us how from the beginning Paul was held in esteem, and yet was also in the storm of controversy: "Our beloved brother Paul wrote to you according to the wisdom given him, speaking of [the time of salvation] as he does in all his letters. There are some things in them hard to understand, which the ignorant and unstable twist to their own destruction" (2 Pet 3:15-16).

People often criticize Paul. Some accuse him of redesigning Christianity for his own purposes, away from the simple teaching of Jesus. Others are annoyed by some of his statements about women. He requires them to wear veils at worship (1 Cor 11:2-16) and he tells them to be silent in the churches (1 Cor 14:34). Such statements seem not to show respect for women and to put them into inferior positions. Similarly, on the topic of human sexuality, Paul seems to have minimal respect for marriage. He says it is better to marry than to burn with passion, but he prefers celibacy (1 Cor 7:8-9). Finally, most of the letters of Paul have strong directives from him, often with explicit assertions of his authority and with little room for discussion on the part of his readers.

Certainly Paul is a strong personality and his letters indicate that people either loved him or hated him, but were scarcely ever neutral or indifferent toward him. Yet we must appreciate that he addressed all of his letters to specific problems of specific communities and often in the heat of battle. His occasionally strong statements need to be kept in context, need to be properly interpreted, and must be balanced by his total vision of Christianity.

In spite of the difficulties and the controversies surrounding Paul, there are important reasons for studying him. Paul can be described as the first theologian, at least as the first to write down his reflections about the meaning of the risen Christ. The letters of Paul are our earliest written texts in the New Testament, and are the largest body of documents after Luke's combined gospel and Acts of the Apostles. He was the right person for the right time. Raised a Jew in Gentile territory, he was eminently suited for his time to help bridge the gap between Christians of Jewish background and the ever increasing numbers of those of Gentile background. Through his writings Paul offers us concrete examples of how a Christian comes to resurrection faith, changes his or her life by it and lives in ongoing commitment and discovery. It is a gift to us that his strong personality comes through in his letters. That enables him not only to leave abstract teaching, but to embody and express for us in a real, live person the struggles, the joys, the fears and the hopes of Christianity. Listen to Paul's personal excitement about the possibilities of Christianity:

> I regard everything as loss because of the surpassing value of knowing Christ Jesus my Lord. For his sake I have suffered the loss of all things, and I regard them as rubbish, in order that I may gain Christ and be found in him, not having a righteousness of my own that comes

from the law, but one that comes through faith in Christ, the righteousness from God based on faith. I want to know Christ and the power of his resurrection, and the sharing of his sufferings by becoming like him in his death, if somehow I may attain the resurrection from the dead" (Phil 3:8-11).

Sources for Study of Paul

As we study Paul, our information will come from varied sources. One source is, of course, the letters from Paul himself. Scholars are agreed that seven are certainly Paul's. These are Romans, 1 and 2 Corinthians, Galatians, Philippians, 1 Thessalonians and Philemon. Scholarly opinion on Paul's authorship runs the gamut from "probably" to "possibly" for three other letters: Colossians, Ephesians and 2 Thessalonians. There is less likelihood, according to scholars, that Paul wrote 1 and 2 Timothy and Titus, and all agree that Paul did not write Hebrews. Our book will concentrate on the seven universally accepted letters. An appendix will be devoted to Colossians and Ephesians. We will not consider the so-called Pastoral Letters to Timothy and Titus, except where they might offer some historical remembrances of Paul's history, and we will not consider the book of Hebrews.

Another source of information about Paul comes from the Acts of the Apostles. We must use Acts cautiously. Luke writes Acts about twenty or thirty years after Paul, idealizes him beyond his historical character, and uses him, along with all the other persons in Acts, in order to express Luke's own faith message and theology. In Acts, Luke wants to paint a picture of the ideal Christian community spreading universally over the Roman Empire. He glides over many of the differences and debates that were part of the early church. He overlooks the rough and random ways in which the message spread. We must pierce through this interpreted history to capture the historical Paul. A comparison of some descriptions in Acts with Paul's versions of the story will highlight the different pictures we can get and the caution with which we must read Acts.

For instance, Luke says that after Paul's conversion, Paul spent a short time in Damascus and then headed to Jerusalem. He gives the impression that Paul needed to be approved properly by the apostles, thus showing the unity of the church. Barnabas introduced Paul to the entire church in Jerusalem. (See Acts 9:19-30.) Paul, on the other hand, in his own account in Galatians 1:15-24, says that after his conversion he saw no need to go directly to Jerusalem. He did not need the approval of others, since his seeing the risen Christ gave him apostolic authority equal to that of the other apostles. Paul asserts that he did not go to Jerusalem until three years later, and then only met privately with Peter and James. The rest of the church would not know him by sight until fourteen years later.

In another section of Acts, Luke presents Peter as quite open to admitting Gentiles into the church, and Paul as quite agreeable to a compromise that Gentiles not eat meat offered to idols (Acts 15:6-29). Paul, on the other hand, says that in Antioch he had to tell Peter off to his face because Peter was afraid to eat at table with Gentiles (Gal 2:11-14). In Corinth Paul maintained that one could eat meat offered to idols as long as it did not offend another person's conscience (1 Cor 8:1-13). In light of such differences between Paul and Luke, we will use the Acts of the Apostles as a supplementary source. Whenever there is conflict in the portrait of Paul, we will give priority to what

Paul says of himself in his letters over what Luke says about Paul for Luke's own purposes.

A further helpful source for studying Paul is the literature and archaeological information from his time. This helps us know the world around Paul and the people whom he addressed. We will now use these varied sources to present Paul's background and teaching. Before beginning the details about the churches within which Paul labored, we will conclude this introduction with a brief overview of Paul's life and a sketch of his missionary journeys. The arrangement of three missionary journeys is the work of Luke in the Acts of the Apostles. There is some debate over whether Paul would actually have recognized three formal journeys, and it may be that for his own purposes Luke is separating into different visits parts of the unified story traditions about Paul that were preserved in particular cities. However, we do have indications from Paul's own letters that he visited some places more than once and, in any case, Luke is our only source of information for some of the events. We will follow Luke's itinerary except where Paul indicates another sequence.

The dating for Paul's life and journeys is usually derived from the Acts of the Apostles, centering on the events that can be coordinated with outside history, but even this process gives only approximation. For instance, one fairly firm date is the term of office of the proconsul, Gallio, in Corinth (1 Cor 18:12-17), which we know to have lasted less than one year, but even here there is debate placing that year somewhere between 50 and 53. Such dating tells us at least that Paul's writings are the earliest in the New Testament. We will use approximate dates, not only to sketch a sequence of events, but also to help show their interrelationship with each other.

Overview of Paul's Life

Our apostle was born in Tarsus in Cilicia (modern southeastern Turkey), probably ten or fifteen years after the birth of Jesus. He was raised a Jew and bore the Jewish name, Saul. Since he also lived among Gentiles, he bore the Gentile name, Paul. He wrote to the Philippians something about his early years: "[I was] circumcised on the eighth day, a member of the people of Israel, of the tribe of Benjamin, a Hebrew born of Hebrews; as to the law, a Pharisee" (Phil 3:5).

The Acts of the Apostles tells us that Paul was trained for a time in Jerusalem in the theology of the Pharisees by the famous rabbi Gamaliel (Acts 22:3). No doubt it was his heritage that led Paul to be concerned, as we shall see, about the relevance of Jewish tradition for Christianity. The strong concern of the Pharisees with proper living of the law would lead Paul to later considerations of the place of the law in light of the resurrection of Jesus. Nevertheless, unlike the Pharisees of the Holy Land, Paul was open to Gentiles, for he came from a thriving Gentile city: "I am a Jew, from Tarsus in Cilicia, a citizen of an important city" (Acts 21:39). On the trade route between Syria and Asia Minor, Tarsus was prosperous and cultured. It was like a university city in which people liked to discuss philosophy and liberal arts. They held their own, even against such famous cities of learning as Athens. Thus, Paul would also eventually be concerned about the meaning of Christianity for these Gentiles.

It may very well be that Paul also had some formal training in the Greek culture within which he lived, for Jews in the cities of the empire often attended the schools and had training in athletics and rhetoric. One of the hallmarks of a Greek city was the gymnasium. Though it was a place of exercise, as the Greek word indicates, it also became the social, civic and education center. In the cities of Asia Minor, such as Tarsus, the gymnasium took on central importance for daily life. The building usually had an open courtyard surrounded by a colonnade, with meeting rooms along one side. These would serve, among other things, as classrooms for the children. Instruction consisted primarily of reading and writing, achieved mostly through the copying and memorizing of standardized texts, such as the epics of Homer. Education was uniform throughout all the Greek cities and everyone shared a common treasury of poems, stories and speeches which they had memorized. Paul would have learned here some of the quotations from Greek writings that found their way into his letters.

Higher education consisted mostly of rhetoric. It was available mostly to young men, though women were not totally excluded, and there are classical texts of rhetoric either authored by women or mentioning women studying the discipline. The students learned the structures of speech, manner of delivery, and models that could be used for various circumstances. Well-crafted public speaking was the sign of a polished and educated person and even the general public knew how to judge plays, recitations and public lectures. All the major philosophical schools were attracted to the principles of rhetoric. Although later on he downplayed these principles as external show (1 Cor 2:1-5), Paul nevertheless learned and even used them when they were helpful. No doubt his audiences sometimes judged him on such principles, even as they judged others. Thus, this part of his early education would also have been significant for Paul's later career.

A CHRONOLOGY OF PAUL'S LIFE

(Dates are approximate)

10	Birth of Paul in Tarsus Possible training under the Pharisee Gamaliel
34	Conversion near Damascus
34-37	Preaching around Arabia (Nabatea) and Damascus
37	Short private visit with Peter and James in Jerusalem
38-46	Invitation to Antioch from Barnabas Missionary activity in Syria and Cilicia
47-48	Possible first missionary journey (into Asia Minor)
49	Visit to Jerusalem "fourteen years later" Council of Jerusalem
50-52	(Second) missionary journey (Asia Minor and Greece) Gallio episode in Corinth Thessalonian correspondence
52-57	(Third) missionary journey (Asia Minor and Greece) Corinthian correspondence mostly from Ephesus Imprisonment in Ephesus and possible correspondence to Galatia, Philippi, and Philemon
57	Letter to the Romans from Corinth
58	Visit to Jerusalem with collection for the poor Arrest and appeal to Caesar
59-60	Sea voyage to Rome interrupted by shipwreck off Malta
62	Imprisonment in Rome Possible letter to the Colossians and Ephesians Death under Roman emperor Nero

Paul's Christian thinking began in his conversion near Damascus about the year 34. He was not a wicked man. In fact he was quite religious, but he could not see how a crucified Jesus could be what Christians were claiming. Neither could he understand how God's gift of the law could be moved from center stage as the response to God's benevolent involvement in the history of Israel. He persecuted Christians out of good conscience—perhaps overzealous, but striving to wipe out a threat to his religion. As Paul himself put it: "You [Galatians] have heard, no doubt, of my earlier life in Judaism. I violently persecuted the church of God and was trying to destroy it. I advanced in Judaism beyond many among my people of the same age, for I was far more zealous for the traditions of my ancestors" (Gal 1:13-14). But new light dawned as Paul saw the risen Christ and thus came to see why his followers made claims that Jesus was truly Lord: "[Christ] appeared to Cephas [Peter], then to the twelve. Then he appeared to more than five hundred brothers and sisters at one time, most of whom are still alive, though some have died. Then he appeared to James, then to all the apostles. Last of all, as to one untimely born, he appeared also to me" (1 Cor 15:5-8).

As zealous for Christ as he was formerly zealous for Judaism, Paul preached for about three years around and in Damascus. When he received threats because of his preaching, he was lowered in a basket from the walls of the city and escaped for a private visit with Peter and James in Jerusalem. Soon after, he received an invitation from Barnabas to join him in Antioch in Syria, where the followers of Christ were first called "Christians." Paul quickly moved out from this home base to bring the good news to the Gentiles and, so, begins what Acts describes as the first of his three missionary journeys. While the chronology of the visits may not have been exactly as Luke describes, the first visits were no doubt into Asia Minor. Acts mentions the regions of Cyprus, Pamphylia, and Pisidia, and then the towns of Iconium, Lystra and Derbe. Acts mentions that at a later time Paul also visited the more northern regions of Asia Minor. There is debate over exact boundaries, but somewhere in this area are the recipients of Paul's letter to the Galatians.

The accomplishments of Paul and Barnabas, both in Antioch and in Asia Minor, led to the influx of great numbers of Gentiles into the church and growing friction between Antioch and the Christians of Jewish background in Jerusalem. Around the year 49, Antioch sent Paul and Barnabas to Jerusalem to resolve the conflict. Based on Luke's description we have come to call this the Council of Jerusalem. In Galatians Paul says that the Jerusalem church sent him out with blessings to preach to the Gentiles and asked only that he remember their poor. On that basis Paul set out again to preach, and also began an extensive collection from his new churches for the poor in Jerusalem.

The more extensive of Paul's journeys are what Luke describes as two into Greece. After passing through Asia Minor around the year 50, Paul sailed from the famous city of Troy into the area of northern Greece called Macedonia and founded the churches of Philippi and Thessalonica. Forced by persecution to leave the area quickly, he travelled south, failing to found a church in Athens, but then doing so successfully in Corinth. The Thessalonian correspondence was likely written from Corinth around this time. Then Paul sailed back to the Holy Land and Antioch, founding the church in Ephesus on the way.

Paul's last travels through Asia Minor and Greece—in what Luke describes as the third journey—provide the occasions for his major letters. Paul revisited Ephesus, making it his base for over two years. From here we have his Corinthian correspondence from about the years 52-56. Paul tells the Corinthians more details about his missionary adventures, giving more information than that found in the Acts of the Apostles.

> [Compared to others I have had] far greater labors, far more imprisonments, with countless floggings, and often near death. Five times I have received from the Jews the forty lashes minus one. Three times I was beaten with rods. Once I received a stoning. Three times I was shipwrecked; for a night and a day I was adrift at sea; on frequent journeys, in danger from rivers, danger from bandits, . . . danger in the city, danger in the wilderness, danger at sea, danger from false brothers and sisters; in toil and hardship, through many a sleepless night, hungry and thirsty, often without food, cold and naked (2 Cor 11:23-27).

If some of these trials not mentioned in Acts include imprisonment in Ephesus, then Paul may have written the letters to the Philippians and to Philemon also during these years, and possibly the letter to the Colossians.

After his lengthy stay in Ephesus, Paul passed through the churches in Macedonia and continued on to Corinth, where he then wrote his great letter to the Romans, about the year 57. Then he revisited the Macedonian communities, sailed to Miletus near Ephesus to say farewell to the Ephesian leaders and returned to Jerusalem with his collection for the poor. Acts tells us that Paul was arrested in Jerusalem, used his Roman citizenship to appeal to the emperor for a hearing and was sent to Rome. Despite shipwreck near Malta, he eventually arrived at Rome where tradition tells us he was beheaded about the year 62. Thus did Paul reach the completion of his most ardent desires:

> I regard everything as loss because of the surpassing value of knowing Christ Jesus my Lord. . . . I want to know Christ and the power of his resurrection, and the sharing of his sufferings by becoming like him in his death, if somehow I may attain the resurrection from the dead (Phil 3:8-11).

The World of Paul

Christianity did not develop in a vacuum. Paul recognized that Christianity needed to address itself to the questions and concerns of its day: "To the Jews I became as a Jew, in order to win Jews. . . . To those outside the law [to the Gentiles] I became as one outside the law . . . that I might win those outside the law" (1 Cor 9:20-21). We will have a better appreciation of Paul's letters if we understand the world in which he lived.

Paul was a city person and his world was predominantly urban. Though there were regional differences, all the major cities where Paul preached and wrote were united by the common languages and cultures of Greece and Rome. There was the more recent Roman legal and political organization over all of the empire, but there was still the art, literature and philosophy of the preceding Greek empire which Rome adopted. Paul redesigned Christianity from the simple message of Jesus, not to change its essence, but to adapt it from a rural, Jewish setting to this urban, Gentile culture. The cities were as cosmopolitan then as they are now.

Urban Social Classes

There were varied classes of people and some chance for social and economic mobility, at least within the mid-

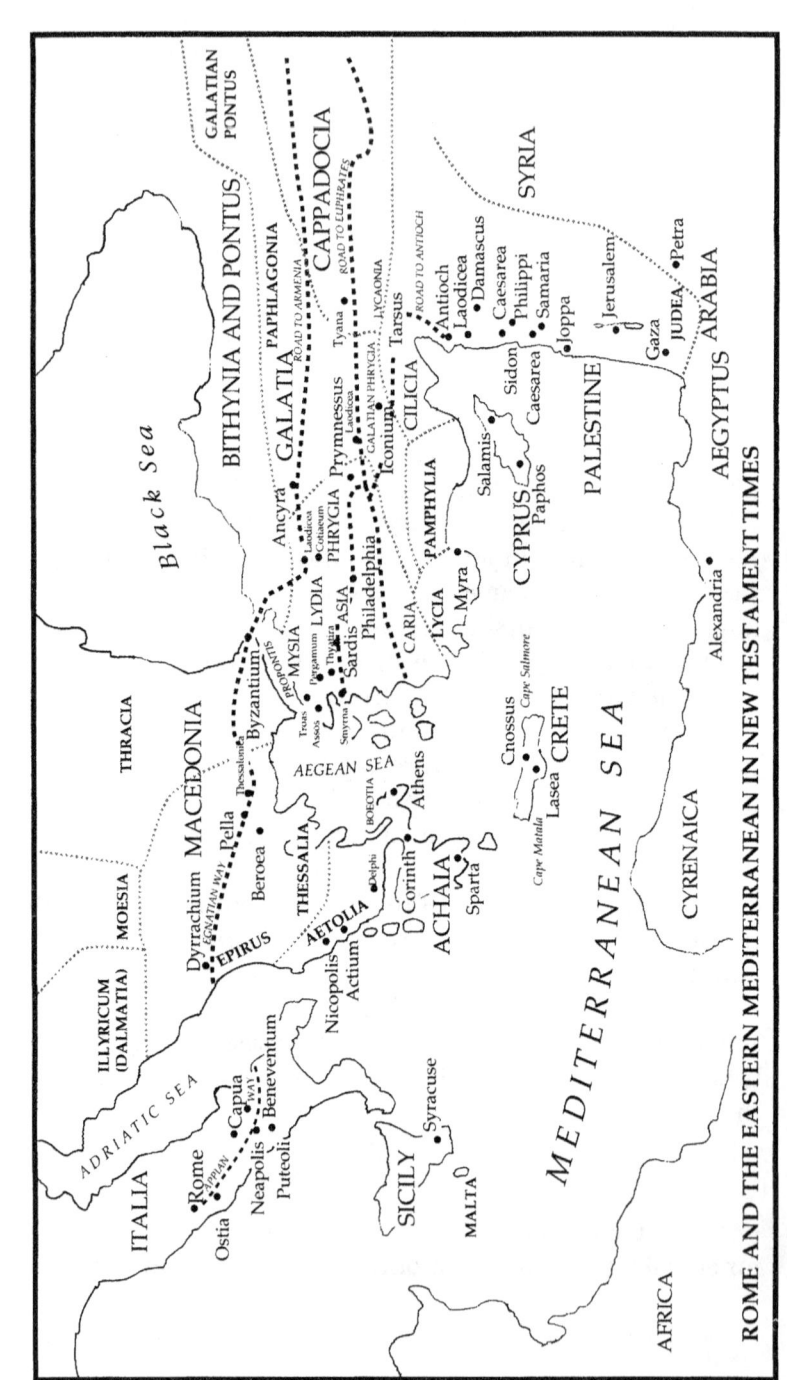

ROME AND THE EASTERN MEDITERRANEAN IN NEW TESTAMENT TIMES

dle and lower classes, and with the help of patrons. The very exclusive upper class comprised the distinguished families of the city of Rome who extended themselves into the empire as some of the administrators or military commanders. On the next level were the local aristocracy composed of those with property and capital for manufacture and trade. Then there were the small landowners, the craftsmen and the shopkeepers. As a tentmaker, Paul himself would fit into this category. Next came the freed men and women who were able to move out of slavery, which was, finally, the lot of the lowest class.

People ended up in slavery through captivity from war, through kidnapping by slave hunters, because of debt, or by being born of slaves. The economic structures of the empire were built upon the system of slavery, which made it difficult to eradicate the practice without creating social upheaval. There was also a difference between the treatment of slaves who were used simply like beasts of burden in farms, mines, and other heavy construction work, and slaves who were members of households. These latter often had administrative tasks, travelled for their masters on business, signed legal contracts and earned money for their own use. Such slaves also had the security of a home and basic necessities, so much so that often, when a slave had the means to purchase freedom, he or she as a freed person then pledged self to the former master or to a patron in order to receive the basics of survival. All this complexity helps explain why Paul did not press for the elimination of slavery, though it does not diminish the immorality of the system. The centrality of slavery leads Paul to devote much ethical consideration to the relationship of master and slave and to offer at least the principles that will eventually eliminate it altogether. The prominence of slavery also explains why Paul uses slave imagery to speak about sin, freedom vocabulary to talk about salvation, and free commitment to Christ as a way to describe the consequence of our liberation.

As part of this intricate Roman system of classes, women were usually expected to hold subordinate positions and were generally expected to assume household tasks. Nevertheless, there was some mobility for them from one class to another, and women in the upper classes sometimes achieved independent prestige in business or in social circles. These women usually inherited wealth and its accompanying power and, while they were few, they were prominent. Paul makes mention on occasion of such women who supported him, who provided their homes as meeting places for the Christians, or who became leaders in their church. Though the practice of Paul's churches was not immune to all the male dominance of the surrounding culture, there were moments of breakthrough in which women achieved better status as Christians than they had in Greco-Roman society.

The Jews generally found themselves also within all the classes of Greek society, having settled widely within these territories from as far back as 587 B.C.E., when the Babylonians destroyed Jerusalem and sent many of the Jews into exile. In general, they were an accepted part of the Roman Empire and participated actively in city life, though they were not always fully understood and sometimes shunned behavior that they could not accommodate to their beliefs. For example, the Jews found it offensive to offer incense to the emperor, though they made it a point to express respect for his authority. They also found it difficult to enter military service, since it created obstacles to their Sabbath worship and dietary laws. They were also uncomfortable with contributing to the support of the local temples. While these particular traits sometimes raised hostility from the society around them, generally they were tolerated. The Romans even occasionally granted formal exemptions from such practices and allowed the Jews to send tax money to Jerusalem for the support of the Temple which had been rebuilt after the Exile.

The gathering places for Jews in the cities of the empire were the synagogues, which served not only as places of worship, but also as schools and community centers. They also provided places of contact for visitors to a city and for travelers in search of work. Paul, who was a tentmaker, could establish contact with others in his trade, when he reached a new city on his journeys, and they could help him secure his means of support. Thus, if Acts is historically accurate, Paul on his journeys went first to the synagogues to facilitate his livelihood as well as to find a ready audience for his preaching.

There was probably a wider audience for Paul in the synagogues than just the Jews. The strong moral standards of the Jews and their monotheism also attracted Gentiles toward the religion, and the Jews in the empire were much more open to converts than were those in Jerusalem. Thus, there were frequently Gentile sympathizers worshiping with the Jews in their synagogues. Not all these Gentiles formally converted to Judaism. Those who did were called proselytes and they underwent official initiation into the religion, with the men also receiving circumcision. Those who did not were called God-fearers and they shared in Sabbath worship or other Jewish activities without becoming Jews. Thus, through the synagogue Paul's preaching reached beyond the Jews to begin touching even the Gentile world of the empire.

Such were the cities of the empire in which Paul preached. He saw his task as one of breaking down the barriers of class and culture. His churches were of mixed

Roman gymnasium of Sardis.

social status and his letters addressed the problems associated with their achieving a genuine sense of unity. Paul's letter to Philemon is a tiny example of the makeup and the problems of his urban communities. To begin with, the letter shows that Paul's churches were household churches, i.e., small communities that met in the larger homes made available by one of their group. The household church was also so named, not only because of the building, but because the household members themselves were the core of the community. The Roman Empire saw itself as one large family composed of smaller households. Each household was composed, not only of a couple and their children, but also of extended family and of other families, friends and associates who were involved in the agriculture, commerce, craft, or other business by which the household survived. Wealthier households had freed persons and slaves as well. Very often these varied groups of people lived in the household, in a number of buildings on wealthy estates or in varied apartments or rooms in simpler households.

Thus, the household was a large social unit and the place of business, some social life, and daily conversation. Paul would have worked out of such households as a coworker, using the occasions as opportunities to preach as well. Frequently, when the master of the house converted to Christianity, the entire household followed. In any case, the household became the base for a church. Certainly, one of Paul's concerns was to foster true unity among all the members and classes of a household and also to address the problems that would arise when not all the members became Christian. In the letter to Philemon we see an example of the household church and Paul's concerns. Philemon and his wife, Apphia, are certainly small landowners and perhaps even of the aristocracy. They are

Christians and head a household church. For one reason or another, one of their slaves has run away, but under Paul's influence has become a Christian. Paul pleads with them to receive back the slave, Onesimus, in a new relationship: "[Onesimus] was separated from you for a while, so that you might have him back forever, no longer as a slave but more than a slave, a beloved brother" (Philemon 15-16). Paul does not call for elimination of the social structures, but he implies a principle that can effect radical change. In his letter to the Galatians he made the principle explicit: "There is no longer Jew or Greek, there is no longer slave or free, there is no longer male and female; for all of you are one in Christ Jesus" (Gal 3:28).

More than to the social structures of the Roman Empire, the teaching of Paul was directed to the ideas and concerns that permeated these cities rich with Greek thought. In general, this thinking sought answers to the deep questions about the meaning of life. Answers were sought in both philosophy and religion. Let us first discuss the philosophies.

Greek Philosophy

Greek philosophy had been flourishing for at least four hundred years before Paul. Philosophic discussion was, of course, prevalent among the aristocracy in important centers like Athens and Tarsus, but it was an important topic in all the cities of the empire and, in popularized version, was part of the conversation at all levels of society. A common issue among all the schools of philosophy was to describe what the world was really like and how to live according to this reality. They differed, though, in their answers to questions such as: "Who or what was at the origin of it all; how did this affect human nature, and what is the well-lived life conformed to this nature?"

One of the prominent ancient philosophers was Plato, though by the time of Paul his formal and theoretical reasoning was losing appeal in favor of more concrete and practical ethical considerations. Nevertheless, his influence was still present and Paul needed to address his ideas. We can get a sense of Plato's thoughts through the following summary presented as a fictitious colloquy of Plato to his disciples:

> I will remain ambiguous in talking about gods or even one God, but I would at least say that there is an unchanging, absolute and eternal spiritual world governed by what I would call the Good. All of our material world is not real, but is a shadow of the real world which is spiritual. Our real nature is the soul, but it is trapped in our body from which at death we hope to escape. In the meanwhile human reason is a faculty of our soul and is the way we come to know and contact the spiritual world and the Good which governs it. If we really want to be happy, then, we must live by reason. We must be educated in virtue in such a way that it causes us to moderate our emotions and to control irrational desires of our body. My motto is "Know thyself." All happiness comes from this deepest kind of self-knowledge.

Paul would encourage the searching of the Platonists and their realization that there is more to this world than material reality. He even wrote to the Romans that human reason is a way of coming into contact with the absolute Good, but of course he gave that Good the name of God: "What can be known about God is plain to them [human beings], because God has shown it to them. Ever since the creation of the world his eternal power and divine nature, invisible though they are, have been understood and seen through the things he has made" (Rom 1:19-20). But Paul had also to temper the Platonists. They were too pessimistic about the body and the material world. He wrote to the Corinthians; "If Christ is proclaimed as raised from the dead, how can some of you say there is no resurrection of the dead? ... [Our body] is sown in weakness, it is raised in power" (1 Cor 15:12, 43). The Platonists were also too optimistic about self-knowledge. Paul wrote likewise to the Corinthians: "If you think that you are wise in this age, you should become fools so that you may become wise. For the wisdom of this world is foolishness with God" (1 Cor 3:18-19).

Of course, Platonism was not the only view of reality with suggestions about how to be happy. The following is a summary presented as the discourse of a fictitious Stoic:

> I, too, will remain ambiguous about whether I am speaking of a personal God, and I will agree with the Platonist that there is indeed a power over all of this world. But I would not agree that this material world is but a shadow or that my body is just a prison for my soul. The real world is all of nature around me. My human reason does indeed put me in contact with the absolute Spirit that governs everything, but this absolute Spirit is one with nature and with my human nature. In fact, the absolute Spirit is bringing all of creation to a predetermined end by fire, so that it can start all over again. If I want to be truly happy, then I will seek with my reason how to act according to nature as it has been predetermined by the absolute Spirit. There is no point in fighting what has been arranged or in letting my emotions get the best of me. My motto is,

A drawing of the Stoa of Attalos based on the reconstructed Stoa presently in the ancient public square and marketplace of Athens. It was from such a stoa, or covered portico, where the philosophers walked up and down while discussing their theories, that the name Stoic derived.

"Take each day as it comes." If I am in a happy situation, then I should enjoy it to the hilt. If I am in tough times, then I must grin and bear it.

Paul would have to temper Stoicism with his Christian insights into a personal God, into an eternal afterlife, and into an active love of others rather than passive self-interest, but he affirmed their shadowy insight into divine providence and their glimpses into the unity of the human race and of all of creation. If we listen to what he told the Corinthians, we see that he especially liked the Stoic concern for self-discipline in ethics, for his words are practically borrowed from the slave, Epictetus, who became a famous Stoic philosopher: "Do you not know that in a race the runners all compete, but only one receives the prize? Run in such a way that you may win it. Athletes exercise self-control in all things; they do it to receive a perishable wreath, but we an imperishable one" (1 Cor 9:24-25).

Every society has its outsiders or counter-culture. The Greek philosophers had theirs in the Epicureans, who might sum up their views as follows:

> I am weary of deciding who better describes reality. I have decided that the gods have no interest in the world, which therefore continues in existence through the random movement of atoms. Happiness, therefore, should not be an effort to reason out what is good or a struggle to do it. Rather, it consists in withdrawing from society and getting as much pleasure as we can among our small circle of friends. My motto is, "Eat, drink and be merry, for tomorrow we die."

In Thessalonica Paul found something to affirm even in the easygoing style of the Epicureans, though, of course, he had other purposes in mind: "We urge you [to love one another] more and more, to aspire to live quietly, to mind your own affairs, and to work with your hands . . . so that you may behave properly toward outsiders and be dependent on no one" (1 Th 4:10-12). Still, Paul warned the Corinthians about Epicurean hedonism: "If the dead are not raised, 'Let us eat and drink, for tomorrow we die.' Do not be deceived: 'Bad company ruins good morals'" (1 Cor 15:32-33).

As important as philosophy was to the culture of Paul's cities, it was centered on the individual and gave little sense of community. To those alienated in the society—especially the freed persons and the slaves, but even others who were uprooted from their native lands—philosophy brought no sense of belonging or of salvation. Since the state religions were in decline, some people turned toward magic, many others toward what are called mystery religions. The magic was a way to get control over life or to influence the powers who did have control. One sought horoscopes, cast spells, or called in other ways on the spirit world to intervene in need. The Galatians and Colossians were both tempted to such practices: "Now that you have come to know God, or rather to be known by God, how can you turn back again to the weak and beggarly elemental spirits? How can you want to be enslaved to them again?" (Gal 4:9).

Mystery Religions

Many more people were attracted to the mystery religions, so called because they had secret rituals reenacting the myth of a god who offered a feeling of salvation to those admitted to the rite. These religions in large part came from the Orient. Almost all of them originated out of ancient civilizations and their concerns for food and drink.

Early humans came to tie the seasons of nature with cycles of events in the lives of their gods. An example of such association is found in the Isis cult which originated in Egypt. According to the myth, Osiris, also known as Serapis, the husband of Isis, is murdered by his brother Seth. Isis discovers his coffin, but Seth recaptures it, dismembers Osiris, and scatters the god widely. Isis retrieves every member and Osiris comes back to life. When Osiris is dead, we are in winter. When Isis searches for him, the season begins to change, and when he returns to life we are in spring and summer and the crops are again alive. We have food until fall, when Seth kidnaps Osiris and the cycle begins again.

The ancients also thought that if they could ritualize these divine events each year, they would encourage their recurrence in the lives of the gods and thus guarantee the life of the crops another year. Gradually, these cults were transformed and spread throughout the Roman Empire. Instead of guaranteeing the life of the crops, the gods were seen as offering life and salvation to the worshipers. One had to know the myth, enter into community with those who preserved it, and celebrate the rituals which reenacted the myth, such as washings, meals and processions. Thus, the people who needed the mystery cults yearned for a savior God, for acceptance by an intimate community, and for sacramental celebrations. Here, too, Paul met their needs, preaching Jesus as the true savior, stressing Christian life as a community in Christ with its initiation by baptism and its sacred meal of the eucharist. Still, Paul also had to encourage them to ethical concerns beyond a *feeling* of salvation and to an open community without secrets.

In many ways, then, Paul addressed the world of his times. He moved Christianity from its Jewish roots to the Gentiles. This would lead to great struggle between Christians of Jewish background and Christians of Gentile background, an issue that we will see recurring in his letters. In moving into the world of the Greco-Roman Empire Paul would also reformulate the Christian message to address the alienation of those who experienced oppression, the ethical concerns of the household churches which he founded, and the searching of both philosophies and religions for the ultimate meaning of life. His message which addressed all these issues was the good news that Jesus is risen and is Lord and that our lives are made whole in him. That message came to Paul on the Damascus road. As one final consideration, before we begin study of the individual churches and their letters, we will look briefly at Paul's conversion experience and the beginnings of his apostolic career.

THE HOLY LAND IN THE NEW TESTAMENT PERIOD

Beginnings of the Mission

The beginning of Paul's apostolic career and the foundations of his missionary work are found in his conversion experience on the road to Damascus. The event is narrated three times in the Acts of the Apostles (9:1-19; 22:3-20; 26:4-18) and is also described briefly by Paul himself in Galatians 1:11-17. There are some differences between Paul and the Acts and, indeed, there are, as we shall see, discrepancies among the three versions of the story in Acts, but the main points converge to give us a solid historical perspective. People usually picture conversion as movement from immoral, sinful existence to a life of holiness, and so they picture Paul's conversion in the same way. Some biblical scholars have interpreted texts like Romans 7:18-20 as Paul's autobiographical description showing his sinfulness before conversion: "I know that nothing good dwells within me, that is, in my flesh. I can will what is right, but I cannot do it. For I do not do the good I want, but the evil I do not want is what I do. Now if I do what I do not want, it is no longer I that do it, but sin that dwells within me."

Other texts of Paul militate against this view of his conversion, showing that Romans 7 must therefore be a general description of the malaise of human beings at large. He writes, for instance, to the Philippians: "If anyone else has reason to be confident in the flesh, I have more:... as to the law, a Pharisee, as to zeal, a persecutor of the church; as to righteousness under the law, blameless" (3:4-6). It appears that Paul was secure and content under the law as a Jew, and lived as a good Jew. So good was he, that he was zealous enough to challenge those who threatened his religion. Paul's conversion, then, was not from a sinful life to a religious life, but rather a major shift from one religious perspective to another. His conversion was sudden, clear and direct: "God, who had set me apart before I was born and called me through his grace, was pleased to reveal his Son to me" (Gal 1:15).

Just what did Paul see? From his own descriptions we do not know. The literal translation of Galatians 1:15 says that God revealed Christ *in* Paul, not just *to* him, so that we are talking about an interior experience. Nonetheless, even in this description, Paul does not want to leave the impression that this experience was purely subjective, simply a psychological change after serious thinking about what Christians were claiming. He says that he received the gospel from no other person, that he was not taught it (Gal 1:11), and that he conferred with no one (Gal 1:16), but only that it came as the revelation of the risen Christ.

The Acts describe the experience as a light and sound manifestation, but the stories are not consistent. According to Acts 9:7, everyone with Paul heard a voice, but saw nothing. According to Acts 22:9, only Paul heard the voice, though they all saw the light (and, in 26:14, all fell to the ground as a result and not only Paul). It seems wise not to take these descriptions too literally, but to see in each story Luke's attempt to show that Paul had some experience that the others did not. The statements of Christ in each story indicate what that experience was: "Saul, Saul, why do you persecute me? . . . I am Jesus, whom you are persecuting" (9:4-5; 22:7-8; 26:14-15). Paul was confronted with the realization that Christ was not dead, but risen and alive; he was present in the Christians whom Paul was persecuting. Whatever Paul saw or heard—if there were any external manifestations at all—he encountered a Christ whose very life was shared as his own. Paul will speak of this as life "in Christ" throughout his writings.

Effects of Paul's Conversion

This encounter with Christ cleared up for Paul the scandal of the cross, which he now saw was not the final reality (1 Cor 1:18-25). It helped him see the continuity of the revelation of God which he knew from his Jewish traditions. His God was still active in history, but now in the raising of Christ (Rom 3:1-26). The kingdom had indeed come, at least in its first fruits in the risen Christ (1 Cor 15:20-28). Finally, the experience of Jesus risen showed Paul that the good things that the law was given to achieve were in fact achieved through Christ (Rom 8:3-4) and that "neither circumcision nor uncircumcision is anything; but a new creation" in Christ (Gal 6:15). These insights from his conversion experience show why Paul from the beginning moved beyond the teaching of the historical Jesus, for in fact, Paul was hardly concerned with the Jesus of history at all, but rather with the risen Christ. He has little usage of Jesus' own vocabulary and teaching about the kingdom of God, and transforms this teaching into the good news about Jesus himself as Lord. For Paul, Jesus himself has become the first product of the kingdom, communicates his life to us, and thereby gradually brings us into the kingdom of God. Thus, instead of repeating Jesus' teaching about living in the kingdom, Paul speaks about living in Christ.

For Paul the encounter with the risen Christ gave him all the essentials for preaching the Christian message and for founding his churches. He tells the Corinthians that it gave him apostolic authority equal to that of the other apostles: "Am I not an apostle? Have I not seen Jesus our Lord?" (1 Cor 9:1). For the same reason, Paul tells the Galatians that after he saw the risen Lord, he felt no need to go immediately to Jerusalem, as if he required permission of the twelve to become an apostle. Rather, he went his own way and visited the others only later, and informally at first (Gal 1:15-20). It was not that Paul impugned previous traditions or teachings, but only that he saw them transformed by a Christ still very much alive and speaking to new times and places. Paul's vision enabled him to experience the risen Christ afresh and thus to adapt the traditions about this Lord to new circumstances and new places, to the world of the Gentiles and to the urban setting of the Roman Empire.

Sensing very strongly his words, "[God] was pleased to reveal his Son to me, so that I might proclaim him among the Gentiles" (Gal 1:16), Paul immediately set about his apostolic mission: "I went away at once into Arabia; and afterwards I returned to Damascus" (Gal 1:17). Arabia, to which Paul travelled, was not the distant country now known as Saudi Arabia, but the kingdom of the Nabateans, an Arab nation, occupying the land south of Damascus and running east of and parallel to the Jordan River and the Dead Sea until it curved southwestward into the Sinai peninsula. Its capital was Petra, famous for its red sandstone royal tombs, and its ruling monarch at the time was King Aretas IV, mentioned by Paul in 2 Corinthians 11:32. Scholars still debate whether Paul went there to preach or to meditate on his conversion experience before beginning his missionary work. Since, according to 2 Corinthians, King Aretas was pursuing Paul, it is likely that Paul was already proclaiming a message and disturbed the king.

The difficulties in "Arabia" brought Paul back to Damascus, in Syria, where he had an opportunity to preach, at least until the governor of King Aretas pursued him and forced him to leave that city also. Damascus is one of the oldest continuously inhabited cities of the world. Like the land of Israel during the Old Testament history, it came under domination of the Assyrians, the Babylonians, the Persians and the Greeks. The Nabateans were able to rule it for a brief period around 85 B.C.E., but by 66 B.C.E. it was a Roman city and part of the Decapolis, the ten-city federation to the east and northeast of the Holy Land. These cities were at this time predominantly Greco-Roman in culture, and Damascus exhibited all the usual architecture and arrangement of such Greek cities, including a temple to its patron deity, Dionysus, the god of wine, and a gymnasium erected as a gift from Herod the Great of Jerusalem.

There was a sizable Jewish community in Damascus. Besides the Jews of Pharisaic persuasion, for whom Paul was originally going to persecute the Christians, there was also a Jewish sect related to the Essene community discovered at Qumran on the Dead Sea in Judea. This was the same monastery that left us the famous Dead Sea Scrolls. The Essenes separated themselves from the rest of the Jews, claiming to live the law more properly and looking forward apocalyptically to the arrival of the Messiah from their community. Apparently some Essenes lived in Damascus. Whether or not Paul was directly influenced by them is hard to say, but there are some common themes between them, such as teaching about the righteousness of God and teaching especially about the final apocalyptic times. As a result of his conversion Paul, of course, made new application of these themes to Christ. He saw Christians as living at the end of the old age of sin and worldly problems, and at the start of the new final age of salvation in Christ (1 Cor 10:11).

Paul's contacts in Damascus would have been Christians as well as Jews, for the stories in the Acts indicate that at his conversion there was already a Christian community in the city. How this community was formed is lost in the past, but it does indicate that Christianity moved outward quickly after the death and resurrection of Jesus. Most likely, these early Christians were of Jewish background, perhaps of Hellenistic Jewish background similar to those who would arrive later, as we shall see, in Antioch in Syria. There is a good possibility that the first Christians in this city came from Galilee, which lay not too far to the southwest. While Paul claimed not to be taught his original revelation by others, and while his vision of the risen Christ seems a privileged kind of event, nevertheless Paul probably began the formulation of his Christian message through the dialogue with both Jews and Christians in Damascus.

Experiences in Antioch

The strongest support for Paul's early apostolic career and the center out of which he seems to have operated extensively was Antioch in Syria. Three years after his conversion he visited privately for a short while with Peter and James in Jerusalem and remained, for the most part, unknown to the rest of the Jerusalem community. Then he returned to the areas he was familiar with, Cilicia, the territory around his hometown of Tarsus, and Syria, the

territory around Damascus and his first mission field. His home base during this time seems to have become Antioch, to which he was invited by Barnabas. While Acts gives a different sequence for the events of Paul which we have narrated, it is helpful in tracing the background of Antioch and the sequence of events that led to Paul's invitation there.

Acts 6 tells of a dispute that arose in Jerusalem between so-called Hellenists and Hebrews. The descriptions do not indicate clearly who are intended, but we can reasonably decipher this. The Hellenists appear to be Christian converts from Judaism, but of the particular background of Hellenistic Judaism; i.e., they spoke Greek as their primary tongue, were comfortable in Greek culture and were willing formerly as Jews to accept Gentile converts into Judaism. These Hellenists probably came out of the Greek-speaking synagogues that we know existed even in Jerusalem, catering to Jews who had emigrated to Jerusalem from outside the Holy Land. Since their perspectives originated in the Diaspora (i.e., Judaism dispersed outside the Holy Land), where there was not much opportunity to get to the Temple regularly, they were less impressed about the importance of the Temple in Jerusalem. When these Jews became Christians they carried over their openness to the Gentiles and their ambivalent feelings toward the Temple. The more radical among them began to feel that Jewish practices no longer had significance for any Christians.

The Hebrews, on the other hand, were the Aramaic-speaking Jews who had become Christians. Their Judaism was indigenous to the land of Israel, was centered on the Temple, and was more resistant to Greek culture and to the acceptance of Gentiles into Judaism. Consequently, after conversion to Christianity, these Hebrew Christians were inclined to maintain the importance of Jewish practices even as an expression of Christian faith. The more conservative among them thought these practices essential for all Christians. In fact, they remained within their synagogues, continued to worship in the Temple, and to practice circumcision and the kosher laws. Earlier verses in Acts, such as 3:1 and 5:12, give some indication of this. The friction that arose between the so-called Hellenists and Hebrews was a debate within the Christian community of Jerusalem, but the seeds of debate had already been planted prior to Christianity by the divergent views within Judaism itself in Jerusalem.

According to Acts 6, the debate came to a head over neglect of the distribution of food to the Hellenist widows. While that may have been the occasion of the outburst, it was a manifestation of the deeper theological differences simmering beneath the surface. These deeper differences came to the fore when one of the newly appointed Hellenist leaders, Stephen, preached against the importance of the Temple for worship (Acts 7). The story in Acts says that this upset the Jews, who then stoned Stephen to death. To add further nuance, while the sermon was no doubt upsetting to Jews, it was also probably upsetting even to the Christian group that Acts calls the Hebrews. While these particular Christians would not have reacted as violently as did the Jews, they would nevertheless have disagreed with the sermon that was representative of the most radical part of the Christian group that Acts calls the Hellenists.

Stephen was killed by Jews who found his criticism of the Temple threatening. (Acts 8:1 says that Paul was also involved. We are not sure whether this is historical or simply Luke's way to introduce Paul into the book. At this point Paul, as a good Jew, would have opposed Stephen's radical rejection of all Jewish practices.) The conflict then broadened quickly: "A severe persecution began against the church in Jerusalem, and all except the apostles were scattered throughout the countryside of Judea and Samaria." (Acts 8:1). Apparently only the radical Hellenist Christians had to flee. The Hebrew Christians, while sometimes criticized by the Jews as in the early chapters of Acts, remained largely tolerated in their Aramaic-speaking Jewish synagogues, since their Christian faith did not diminish the importance of their Jewish practices. That is why Luke says that the church in Jerusalem scattered *except the apostles,* who would have been Hebrew Christians.

The persecution was a blessing in disguise, for it opened Christianity to a massive entrance of Gentile converts. The fleeing Hellenists went to Antioch and there began openly to recruit Gentiles into their Christian community:

> Now those who were scattered because of the persecution that took place over Stephen traveled as far as Phoenicia, Cyprus, and Antioch, and they spoke the word to no one except Jews. But among them were some men of Cyprus and Cyrene who, on coming to Antioch, spoke to the Greeks also, proclaiming the Lord Jesus. And the hand of the Lord was with them, and a great number became believers and turned to the Lord (Acts 11:19-21).

With the influx of the Gentiles, that many more Christians were questioning the relevance of Jewish practices for Christian faith. The debate that began between groups in Jerusalem now became a debate between Jerusalem and Antioch. In Antioch, Christians of Gentile background sided with Hellenist Christians against the Hebrew Christians in Jerusalem who still called for Jewish practices as part of the expression of Christian faith.

Acts 11:22-26 tells us:

> News of [the Antioch church] came to the ears of the church in Jerusalem, and they sent Barnabas to Antioch. When he came and saw the grace of God, he rejoiced, and he exhorted them all to remain faithful to the Lord with steadfast devotion; for he was a good man, full of the Holy Spirit and of faith. And a great many people were brought to the Lord. Then Barnabas went to Tarsus to look for Saul, and when he had found him, he brought him to Antioch.

The Jerusalem church likely became concerned about what was going on in Antioch and dispatched Barnabas to try to mediate between the Hebrew Christians and the radical Hellenist/Gentile view. Barnabas, at least at the beginning, became convinced of the Hellenist/Gentile approach, remained in Antioch, became a leader there and invited the now converted Paul to join him. Thus, the apostle was drawn into the debate that would grow over the next years and be an ongoing problem in his churches and in his writings. The problem became severe as Paul began to gather more and more Gentiles into his churches. Before discussing the next phase of this crisis, we turn to the start of Paul's major missionary undertakings. Antioch became the base of Paul's missionary work and from there he launched what Acts describes as his first missionary journey (Acts 13-14).

It is not surprising that Paul's journeys took him westward. The Roman Empire had provided a relative peace during this time and an elaborate set of roads and pirate-free shipping lanes that made travel safer and interchange between cities easier. The places where Paul preached and the churches that he founded were seaport cities on the trade routes or were the major population centers along the Roman highway system. Antioch in Syria had a significant relationship with these routes. It was the third largest city of the empire, after Rome and Alexandria. Founded as a city of Greek culture about 300 B.C.E., by one of the generals of Alexander the Great just after Alexander's death, it became his capital and continued as capital of the Roman province of Syria, when Rome took over this territory in 64 B.C.E. under Pompey. Augustus enlarged it, and during the time of Jesus the emperor Tiberius and Herod the Great collaborated on a magnificent colonnaded street that made Antioch one of the most beautiful cities of the Roman world and even more influential in commerce. Situated near the frontier of the eastern part of the empire, this cosmopolitan city connected the Orient to the empire through roads from Mesopotamia and the east, roads westward to Tarsus and the rest of Turkey, and routes southward to Damascus and Palestine. Situated on the Orontes River, it also had a seaport on the Mediterranean at Seleucia Pieria.

First Missionary Journey

Paul sailed with Barnabas and others from Antioch's port to the island of Cyprus and then on to the coast and the south-central part of Turkey. Our knowledge of events here is only from Luke and is no doubt colored by his own perspectives and purposes, but we may draw some insights that show Paul's world and provide background and preparation for his later writings. We see, for instance, that Paul works for the most part in the significant cities of the Roman Empire. Cyprus was the third largest island of the

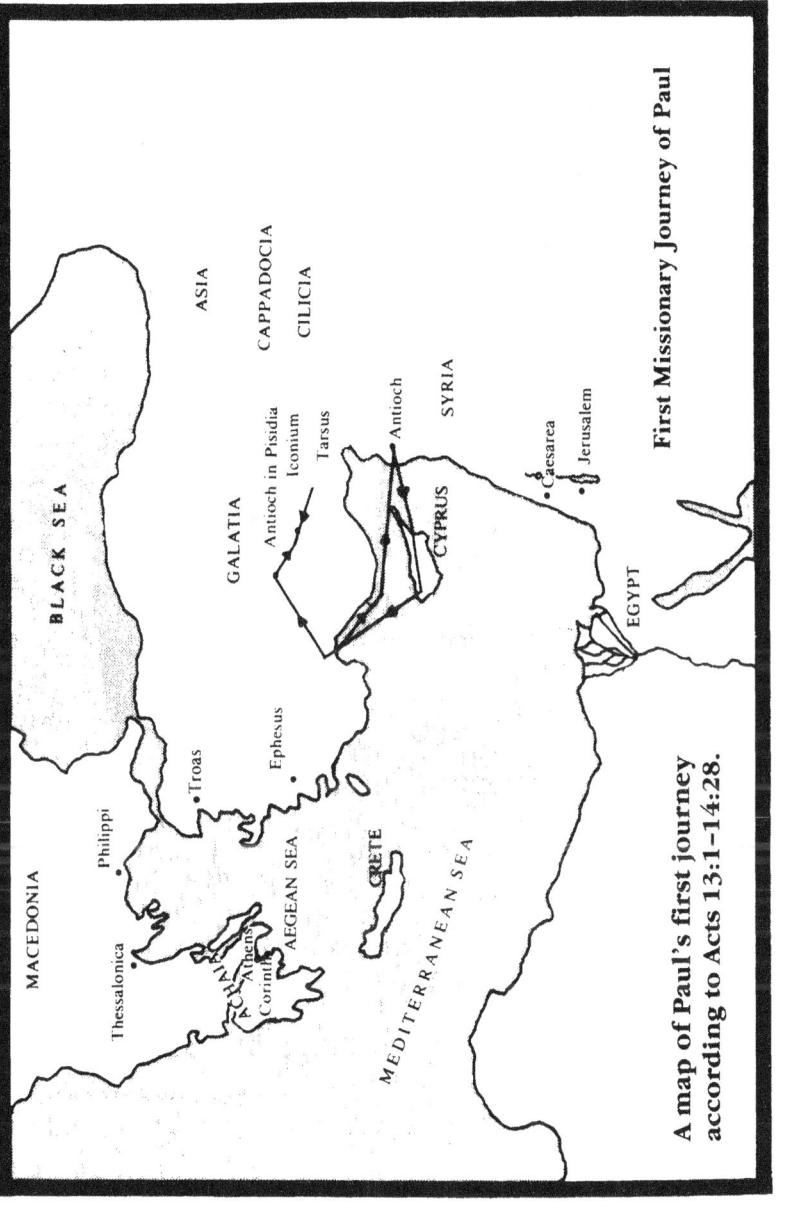

Mediterranean and important for its copper. Perga, on the coast, was the chief city of the southern Roman province of Pamphylia-Lycia. Moving farther north and then southeastward, Antioch (not the one in Syria, but near Pisidia), Iconium, Lystra and Derbe were all strategic border cities between territories, were local centers on the elaborate road system, and were colonized by the Roman aristocracy and military. These cities were on the borders of the territories of Phrygia, Pisidia and Lycaonia. North of these territories was the ethnic area and former kingdom of Galatia. The Romans combined all the territories into one province which they called Galatia. This creates an ambiguity for us today, for we do not know whether Paul's letter to the Galatians was addressed to these southern cities and territories in the province of Galatia or only to the original Galatia of the ethnic, northern area which Paul may have visited on later travels.

In the southern locations there were Jewish communities and we see Paul beginning in the synagogues and ending with the Gentiles. We are not sure if this was the historical pattern of Paul's visits, but it does seem corroborated by Paul's statement that God's power of salvation is "to the Jew first and also to the Greek" (Rom 1:16). Moreover, these stories illustrate the point we made earlier that the synagogues were a way to the Gentiles, for there were Gentile God-fearers and proselytes at these synagogues. Finally, it may be that these stories in Acts describe some of the hardships to which Paul generally refers later on in 2 Corinthians 11:24-27. "Once I received a stoning" probably refers to such an event in Lystra. Paul's hiking from the coast into the mountainous region of these cities, along with hostilities stirred up by Jewish opponents, would make sense of his references to "danger from rivers, danger from bandits, danger from my own people, danger from Gentiles, danger in the city, danger in the wilderness,... hungry and thirsty, often without food, cold and naked."

Having spoken about the first journey of Paul and Barnabas, it is time to return now to the next phase of the dispute over Jewish practices between the Jerusalem church of the Hebrew Christians and the Antioch church of Hellenist and Gentile Christians. Some scholars think that this new crisis occurred even before the Asia Minor journey. They take as strict geography Paul's words to the Galatians that after his first visit to Jerusalem he travelled through Syria and Cilicia and then after fourteen years (from his conversion? from his first trip?) had to return to resolve this dispute (Gal 1:21-2:1). Others build on Luke's version that Paul and Barnabas went to Jerusalem for this purpose *after* their trip through Asia Minor (Acts 15). In either case, the Gentiles had become numerous and the problem enormous. Both the Acts and Paul in Galatians affirm that the crisis was resolved for the moment. The Jerusalem church under Peter and James encouraged Paul in his ministry to the Gentiles and required no Jewish practices from these new converts, but only that they remember the poor in Jerusalem (Gal 2:6-10).

Luke adds other stipulations in Acts 15:12-35, but this was probably a later decision after a further event described by Paul in Galatians 2:11-14. Apparently, Peter visited Antioch shortly after the "Jerusalem Council." Under pressure from what we have been calling the Hebrew Christians, who came from Jerusalem and claimed the support of James, Peter reneged on leaving Gentiles free from circumcision and kosher laws and would not eat at table with Gentiles. Barnabas sided with Peter against Paul in a severe disagreement. Paul never says whether he won or lost that argument, but it is likely that he lost in

Antioch. For after this time Barnabas and Paul parted ways and Paul started on his journeys to Greece with Silas. In the meantime, the Jerusalem church under James devised for the future what it saw as a compromise solution, namely, not to impose on Gentiles any Jewish practices other than what was binding on Gentiles from Old Testament traditions in Leviticus 17-18. These are enunciated by Luke in Acts 15:12-35 as a further result of the Jerusalem Council, although, as we said, they are probably later historically, after Paul left Antioch. The stipulations were that the Gentiles abstain from food offered to idols, from incestuous marriages ("unchastity"), and from food with the blood in it, including animals killed by strangulation.

Thus, four Christian groups seem to have arisen out of the struggles in Antioch. Two were related to those Acts called the Hebrews: (1) an arch-conservative "circumcision party" that demanded that Gentiles follow all Jewish practices, and (2) a moderate conservative group that asked only that the Gentiles compromise on food regulations to allow table fellowship with Jewish Christians. Against these were two views related to those Acts called the Hellenists, now joined also by Gentiles: (1) Paul's moderate view that Jewish Christians could continue Jewish practices while Gentiles were free from all such practices, and (2) a radical group like Stephen's that said Jewish practices were to be eliminated even for Jewish Christians. As Paul began his major journeys through western Turkey and Greece, his writings would reflect the continuing struggle between his law-free gospel for the Gentiles and the demands from the circumcision party that all Jewish practices be imposed even on Gentile Christians.

Thessalonians and Philippians

We mentioned previously that people either loved or hated Paul with his strong personality. In this presentation we consider two churches with which Paul shared deep affection. His letters to the Thessalonians and the Philippians show his desire to maintain and to strengthen those bonds, as well as to address the specific problems of these communities. Both the churches of Thessalonica and Philippi were located in Macedonia, the northeastern part of Greece, and they were the first cities that Paul visited after Asia Minor.

We have indicated that the number of Paul's journeys and the itinerary are not certain. Those who think that Paul visited Asia Minor only after the Jerusalem Council suggest that the stories of Paul's first and second journeys in Acts should be merged, and that Paul first visited those cities in Asia Minor on the way to Greece. According to their perspective, the likely history is that Paul made two major missionary journeys and not three, and that Luke develops three journeys for his own theological purpose of showing the gradual universal spread of Christianity. Those who think that Paul first visited Asia Minor before the Jerusalem

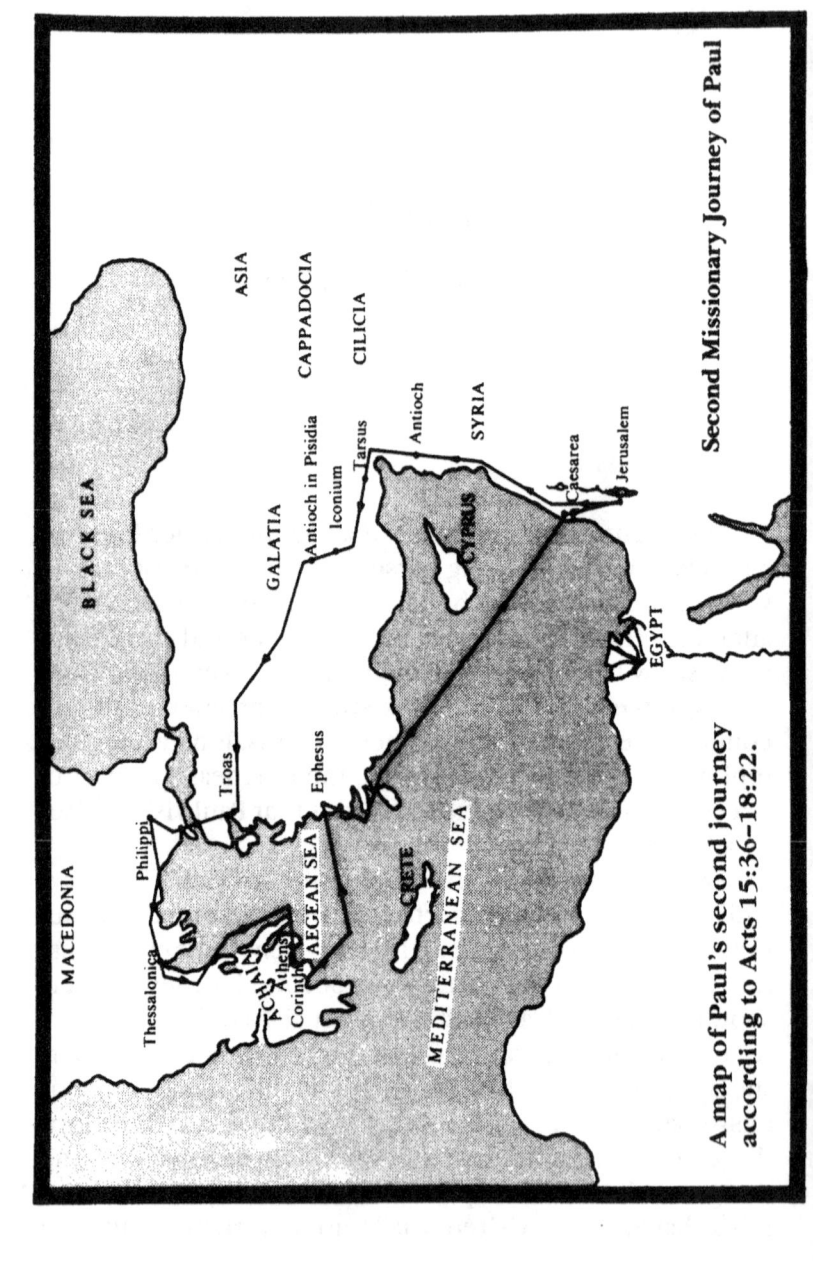

Council contend that Luke's account of three journeys is accurate and that the mention of Derbe, Lystra and Iconium in Acts 16:1-5 is not a doublet of the stories in the earlier chapters, but a second visit on the way to Greece.

In either case, in Acts 16:9-10, Luke describes Paul's inspiration to expand the mission to Greece:

> During the night Paul had a vision: there stood a man of Macedonia pleading with him and saying, "Come over to Macedonia and help us." When he had seen the vision, we immediately tried to cross over to Macedonia, being convinced that God had called us to proclaim the good news to them.

Notice that in this section Luke begins to use the pronoun "we" in his description of the journey, a possible indication that he accompanied Paul, along with Silas and Timothy, or perhaps that he used the travel diary of one such companion. Paul always had coworkers, including women, on his missions. We should, in our study of his churches, give some notice to these unsung heroes.

Paul and his companions sailed from the famous city of Troy to the island of Samothrace and on to Neapolis, the seaport city near Philippi. From here began one of the famous Roman roads which connected all the provinces of the empire. We have an illustration again of Paul selecting the cities because of their accessibility to the major roads. In this case, the Via Egnatia connected northern Greece from the Aegean Sea to the Adriatic. Along this highway were Philippi, where Paul founded his first church in Greece, Amphipolis and Apollonia, through which he passed, and Thessalonica, the capital of Macedonia, to which Paul wrote his first letter.

The City of Thessalonica

Thessalonica was—and in fact still is—the hub of commerce and communication for northern Greece. It was founded about 315 B.C.E. by King Cassander of Macedonia, a general of Alexander the Great who inherited northern Greece after Alexander's death. Cassander named the city after his wife, who was the half-sister of Alexander. In Paul's time, the Romans had declared Thessalonica a "free city," meaning that it had some semblance of autonomy with its own political leaders, called "politarchs" or "city authorities." Throughout Roman occupation the city maintained its Greek character despite the influx of craftsmen, traders, wandering philosophical preachers, soldiers and others from Asia Minor and Italy as well as from other parts of Greece. There was also a sizable Jewish population with its synagogue.

Luke tells us that Paul went with Silas first to the synagogue and preached about three weeks: "Some of them were persuaded and joined Paul and Silas, as did a great many of the devout Greeks and not a few of the leading women" (Acts 17:4). Opposition grew, however, from the Jewish community, so Paul moved to the house of one of his converts named Jason. We see here confirmation of the fact that Christianity developed primarily as a household church, with early Christians meeting in the homes of prominent members of their community. Apparently Paul's success continued after the first three weeks, so that the greatest number of converts came from among the Gentiles. For when Paul later writes the Thessalonians, he mentions that they turned to God from idols (1 Th 1:9).

Pagan worship would have been extensive in Thessalonica, where, among others, the goddess Roma was venerated and where the emperors were honored for their beneficence even to the extent of divinizing them after death. There was in the city a temple to Julius Caesar as a god. Even more prominent than these official cults were the mystery religions. Some devotees met in homes for the rites of Isis and Serapis, which were imported from Egypt. One of the native Greek mystery religions was that of Dionysus, the god of wine. Another, inherited from the nearby island of Samothrace, centered on the god, Cabirus, and his consort and, like most of the mystery religions, ritualized the sexual relations of the deities after kidnapping, death, search and reunion. One can image the debauchery and the drunkenness that comprised the reenactment of the myths of these gods, so that people could feel accepted by a community and feel saved by their gods! Perhaps this is also why Paul would later write the Thessalonians: "This is the will of God, your sanctification: that you abstain from fornication; that each one of you know how to control your own body in holiness and honor, not with lustful passion, like the Gentiles who do not know God" (1 Th 4:3-5).

Eventually, the preaching of Paul and his companions met such opposition that they were forced out of the city. They moved on to Beroea, but the opponents from Thessalonica pursued them until they left for the south. In Athens, Paul sent Timothy back to Thessalonica, fearful that his young community would dissolve under the pressures of persecution. Completing his task, Timothy finally caught up with Paul in Corinth and brought the good news that the church in Thessalonica had persevered. This occasions the letter from Paul, Silas and Timothy to the Thessalonians, praising them for their faith, love and steadfastness, and telling them that they had become an example to Macedonia and to all the rest of Greece.

Problems also arose, however, over Paul's teachings

about the second coming of Christ. The Thessalonians expected this second coming very soon in their own lifetime, an expectation not uncommon in the earliest years after the resurrection of Jesus. In view of that expectation, several problems arose. We can reconstruct what the Thessalonians were probably saying, as we read how Paul responded in his Thessalonian correspondence. No doubt one of the concerns of the community was about those Christians who had died. If the second coming of Christ is very soon, what about those who have already died? Will they miss out on Christ's final victory? Paul had to assure them, "We do not want you to be uninformed, brothers and sisters, about those who have died, so that you may not grieve as others do who have no hope. . . . God will bring with [Jesus] those who have died. . . . We who are alive, who are left until the coming of the Lord, will by no means precede those who have died" (1 Th 4:13-15).

When Paul speaks about the coming of Christ, he draws on images familiar to his social world. The very word which he used in Greek for "coming," *parousia,* was the word used to describe the victory processions of the kings, when they returned to their cities after a successful war and brought back slaves, booty and other war trophies. Often a triumphal arch was built with friezes depicting the battles or the victory procession itself. One famous example is the Arch of Titus which has stone reliefs depicting the victor returning to Rome with the Jewish seven-candle lampstand (the menorah) and with other trophies from the destruction of Jerusalem in 70 C.E. Paul described Christ's final victory over evil in these terms as a victory procession in which Christ will be welcomed by all Christians who will greet him as he arrives with his victorious army:

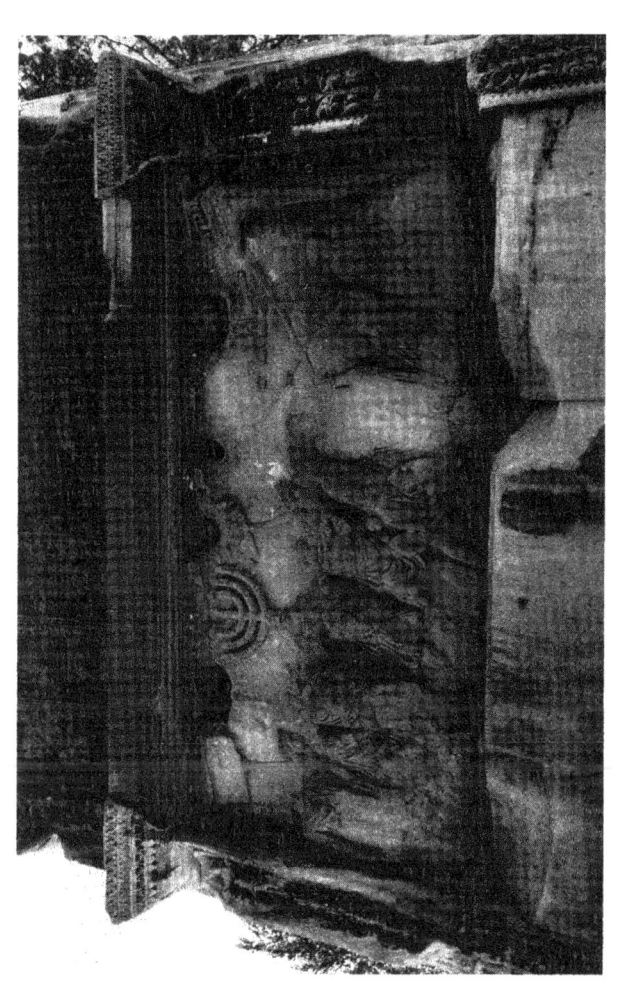

An artist's sketch of a frieze on the Arch of Titus in Rome, celebrating the victory procession (parousia) of the emperor carrying the spoils of victory after the destruction of Jerusalem. Notice the seven branch candelabra taken from the Temple.

> The Lord himself, with a cry of command, with the archangel's call and with the sound of God's trumpet, will descend from heaven, and the dead in Christ will rise first. Then we who are alive, who are left, will be caught up in the clouds together with them to meet the Lord in the air; and so we will be with the Lord forever. Therefore encourage one another with these words (1 Th 4:16-18).

Another concern of the Thessalonians related to eschatology (i.e., theology about the final time of salvation) seems to have been over what the signs were by which they could anticipate and then recognize the second coming of Christ. Paul had to clarify: "Now concerning the times and the seasons, brothers and sisters, you do not need to have anything written to you. For you yourselves know very well that the day of the Lord will come like a thief in the night" (1 Th 5:1-2). We notice here how Paul builds on earlier tradition but applies it to a new situation. Jesus himself gave the example of the thief in the night to speak about the sudden and mysterious arrival of the kingdom of God. Now Paul uses the imagery to speak about the sudden and mysterious completion of the work of the risen Christ.

Apparently several other consequences flowed from their misunderstanding of the second coming of Jesus. Some thought that if the second coming of Christ is very soon, then they did not have any need to keep working. Others seem to have become frightened or anxious about what was going to happen. Still others may have wished for that coming in order to eliminate the problems with which they felt overwhelmed. Paul had words for them all: "We urge you, beloved, to admonish the idlers, encourage the fainthearted, help the weak, be patient with all of them. . . . May your spirit and soul and body be kept sound and blameless at the coming of our Lord Jesus Christ" (1 Th 5:14, 23).

Paul's relationship with the Thessalonians, the nature of some of their problems, and the way in which Paul treats them find parallels in some of the philosophical traditions in this Greek city. While Paul was not a moral philosopher, he seems to have learned from these familiar traditions ways of strengthening the community and his ties with them. Sometimes making use of the household, or conversation in the craftshop, the moral philosopher sought by rhetoric and instruction to bring disciples to a higher life of virtue. The philosopher frequently had to speak frankly and to challenge his hearers in order to bring about change, and often he sought emotional response and commitment as well as rational agreement. Unlike these rhetoricians, Paul realized that it was not simply his instruction that commanded power, nor simply the self-improvement of his hearers that brought moral growth, but the risen Christ and his gift of the Spirit. Nevertheless, the Holy Spirit worked through instruction and also required responsive commitment of the whole person in order to bring about conversion. Paul resembled the philosophers in giving instruction in the household where he worked and in calling his hearers to conversion.

Some philosophers were not harsh, but took the approach of gentle persuasion. Paul renewed his bonds with the community in describing himself much in the fashion of these moral philosophers: "We were gentle among you, like a nurse tenderly caring for her own children.... As you know, we dealt with each one of you like a father with his children, urging and encouraging you and pleading that you lead a life worthy of God" (1 Th 2:7, 11-12). The Thessalonian Christians experienced many of the problems faced by new followers of a philosopher: discouragement at not making faster progress in virtue, alienation from family and friends who did not join the movement, lack of full moral education in the school of thought. Paul stresses solutions similar to those of the philosophers. Besides giving his followers a sense of belonging through the kinship language we have indicated above, he offers himself as a model for imitation (1 Th 1:6), he reminds them of the marvelous deeds they have already accomplished (1 Th 1:7-10; 3:6-7; 4:1, 9-10), and he exhorts them to mutual care (1 Th 4:9-10; 5:12-15).

Some scholars doubt that Paul wrote 2 Thessalonians, since the language, style and theology show some differences from the other letters. But there is, however, also similarity of thought. If Paul wrote the letter, it was probably close upon writing 1 Thessalonians and even uses some of the same phrasing. It is possible that Paul's teaching about eschatology in his first letter led some to press the imminence of their expectations, so that the refusal to work and their idleness worsened. Paul then insisted that the end, though imminent, was not that imminent, since the final conflict against the rebelling forces of evil and against those diametrically opposed to Christ had yet to be achieved (2 Th 2:3-7). He also curtly laid down the principle, "Anyone unwilling to work should not eat. For we hear that some of you are living in idleness, mere busybodies, not doing any work" (2 Th 3:10-11).

The City of Philippi

The Thessalonian correspondence appears to be the only writing we have from Paul's first visit through Greece on what Acts describes as his second journey. The letter to the Philippians would be part of a later correspondence. In order to understand that writing we return now to further consideration of the social world around this first foundation of Paul in Greece. Philippi was a very Roman city in its culture at that time. Named for Philip, the royal father of Alexander the Great, the city was also the site of the defeat of the assassins of Julius Caesar by Octavian (the future Caesar Augustus) and Antony (the future husband of Cleopatra). Octavian and Antony settled their veterans in this colony as a reward for loyalty. Philippi became a miniature Rome, so much so that many of the preserved inscriptions bear Latin names.

There were probably not many Jews in this Roman colony. Acts tells us that Paul and his companions went out to a riverside to a place for prayer on the Sabbath, indicating that there was probably no synagogue in the area. On the other hand, Gentile religions flourished. There was the official Roman religion with temples or statues to Jupiter, Juno, Minerva, Mercury, Mars and other Roman deities. There were also mystery religions, including the cult of Isis and Serapis as in Thessalonica. Acts tells us that Paul cast a demon out of a slave girl who was soothsaying, indicating that perhaps magic and astrology were also in vogue in this city. All in all, there was enough for resistance here, as in Thessalonica, for Paul to remark to the Thessalonians, "Though we had already suffered and been shamefully mistreated at Philippi, as you know, we had courage in our God to declare to you the gospel of God in spite of great opposition" (1 Th 2:2).

In face of that great opposition Paul won over a community and established deep ties of affection. Included among his converts was Lydia, a wealthy woman dealing in purple goods, who welcomed the community to her home and became patroness of a household church. There were other prominent women, such as Syntyche and Euodia, mentioned in the letter to the Philippians as coworkers in founding the church there. Many ties of affection will be evident in the letter to the Philippians. We might also add a further indication: later on when Paul experienced profound troubles with the church in Corinth, he found Philippi a place of refuge and comfort, and made a special trip there in order to gather strength for the Corinthian conflict.

The letter to the Philippians was written later from prison. This has led tradition to assume that Paul writes from Rome, the place of imprisonment mentioned in the Acts of the Apostles. There is also mention, in Philippians 4:22, that members of "Caesar's household" send greetings, which seems to indicate a Roman origin. However, Paul tells of other imprisonments and may refer to one in telling the Corinthians that he "fought with beasts at Ephesus" (1 Cor 15:32). It was also the case that the emperors had slaves, freed persons and other staff in some of the Roman colonies, so that "Caesar's household" can indicate some who became Christians in Ephesus. They may, in fact, have been the soldiers at the prison. If these points are indicative, then Paul wrote Philippians from Ephesus during his last major trip through Asia Minor around the same time as his Corinthian correspondence, all during what Luke describes as the third missionary journey.

Actually, we may have three letters merged into what we now call the one letter to the Philippians. Chapter 4:10-20 seems to be an early note to thank the Philippians for gifts they had sent through Epaphroditus to Paul in prison. It shows the trust that Paul had in the Philippians that he was willing to receive from them gifts that probably even included money. Recall that Paul wrote in several places that he would never take money, but would work for his keep as a tentmaker, so that no one could accuse him of preaching in order to make money. Nevertheless, his confidence that the Philippians would never betray their friendship by such accusations permitted him to accept their gifts. The Philippians also supported his work in Thessalonica (Phil 4:16), in Corinth (2 Cor 11:9), and in his collection for the poor in Jerusalem (2 Cor 8:2-5).

In another letter, found in 1:1 to 3:1 and 4:2-9, Paul expounds further on his suffering in prison. They are for the sake of Christ (1:20) and are both an example for the Philippians (1:29-30) and a sacrifice which Paul makes of himself for them (2:17). We shall see that Paul gives further description of the relationship of suffering to his ministry when he writes to the Corinthians. If suffering does have this role, however, then the Philippians must be willing to suffer as well. They have to struggle against outsiders who are coming in and disturbing the community (1:28). This may be a hint of Jewish Christians imposing views on Gentile-Christian practices, as the third letter fragment will indicate more clearly. There was also strife among some of the leaders (4:2-3) and the need to reestablish unity and harmony in the church. To exhort them to this, Paul quotes what is probably a Christian hymn familiar in their worship:

> Let each of you look not to your own interests, but to the interests of others. Let this same mind be in you that was in Christ Jesus, who, though he was in the form of God, did not regard equality with God as something to be exploited, but emptied himself, taking the form of a slave, being born in human likeness. And being found in human form, he humbled himself and became obedient to the point of death—even death on a cross. Therefore God also highly exalted him and gave him the name that is above every name, so that at the name of Jesus every knee should bend, in heaven and on earth and under the earth, and every tongue

should confess that Jesus Christ is Lord, to the glory of God the Father (Phil 2:5-11).

This hymn not only offers Christ as example for meekness and care for others, but also sums up the most important elements in Paul's theology of Christ, namely, Christ's death and resurrection and his becoming Lord. The clearest understanding of the hymn comes if we see it as the contrast to Adam. In writing to the Corinthians and later to the Romans Paul will explicitly develop this theme of Christ as the new and better Adam. Here the new Adam seems implicitly contrasted with the old Adam. Though that first Adam was in the image of God, he thought it something to be grasped to be as God, and filled himself, refusing the form of a servant and seeking to be like God. Being found in human form he exalted himself, becoming disobedient even unto death, whereby he was humbled and disgraced, losing his reputation before all of creation.

It seems that this letter was brought to the Philippians by Epaphroditus, who had become seriously ill and remained with Paul after he had brought the gifts that occasioned the first of Paul's notes. The Philippians had heard of the illness and were concerned about their brother, so Paul sent him back with this letter, including some words about him which give testimony not only to much affection among friends but also again to the role of suffering:

> I think it necessary to send to you Epaphroditus—my brother and coworker and fellow soldier, your messenger and minister to my need; for he has been longing for all of you, and has been distressed because you heard that he was ill. He was indeed so ill that he nearly died. But God had mercy on him, and not only on him but on me also, so that I would not have one sorrow

after another. I am the more eager to send him, therefore, in order that you may rejoice at seeing him again, and that I may be less anxious. Welcome him then in the Lord with all joy; and honor such people, because he came close to death for the work of Christ, risking his life to make up for those services that you could not give me (2:25-30).

At a later time Paul sent another letter, now found in 3:2-4:1, because problems were increasing in Philippi. The Christians of Jewish background were insisting that even Gentile converts express their faith in Jesus through Jewish practices. It seems that the dispute that had exploded earlier between Antioch and Jerusalem was seeping into the Gentile churches that Paul had founded. It is likely that his opponents in Philippi were people from Jerusalem or people who at least claimed support of the position of the most conservative of the Jewish Christians of Jerusalem, the group we earlier described as the "circumcision party" of the Hebrews. Paul insists that circumcision and the Jewish law must not be imposed on Gentiles as a requirement of Christian practice. He reminds the Philippians that he can boast of Jewish background just as much as the so-called "Judaizers" from Jerusalem, but that circumcision is no longer what counts: "If anyone else has reason to be confident in the flesh, I have more: circumcised on the eighth day, a member of the people of Israel. . . . Yet whatever gains I had, these I have come to regard as loss because of Christ" (Phil 3:4-7). We will see this problem again in the letter to the Galatians.

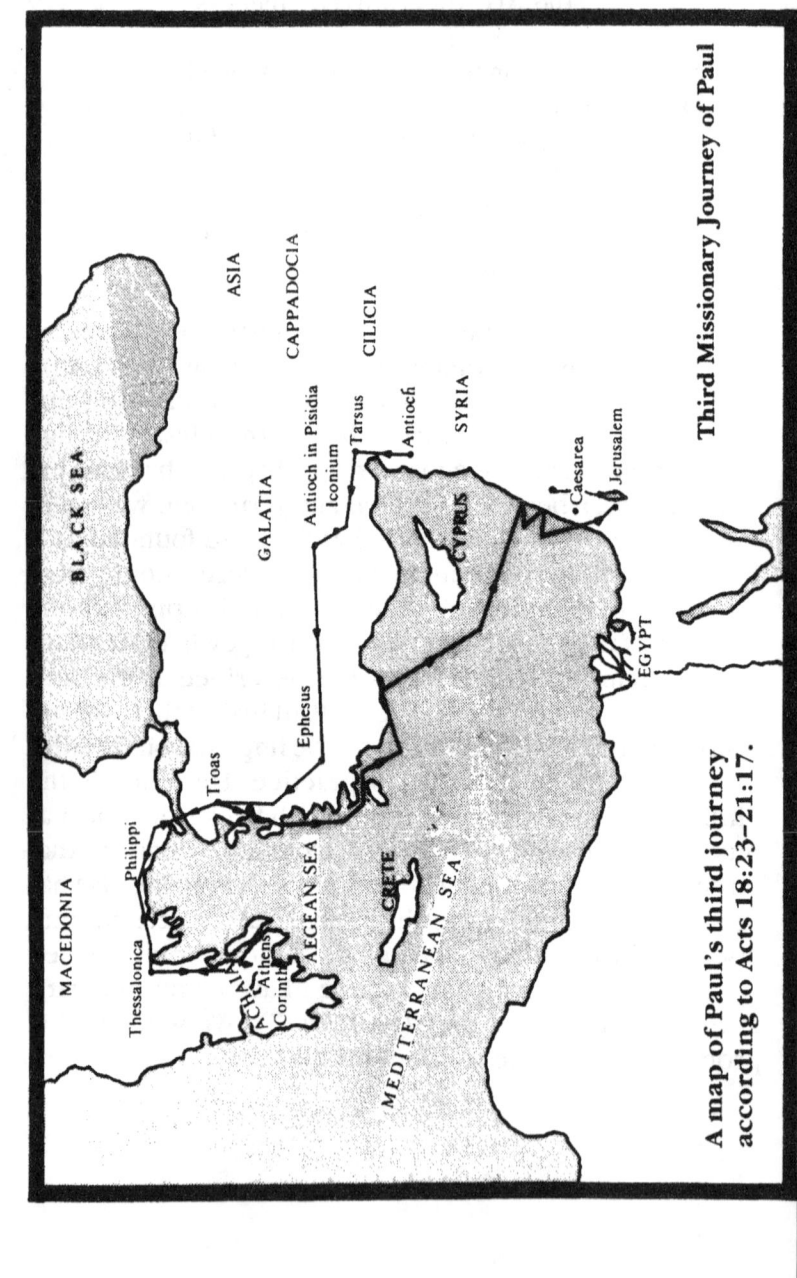

The Church in Corinth

Paul wrote his letters to specific communities almost always to address particular problems or concerns. We can see a good side to the fact that the church in Corinth had so many problems. Were it not for them we would not have Paul's most lengthy correspondence and would be deprived of much of his theology. From the information that we have, Paul spent more time in Corinth than in any other city. According to Luke, after being driven out of Macedonia on his second missionary journey, Paul tried to found a church in Athens, but without success. He moved on to Corinth and stayed for about eighteen months, using this city as his base of operations. He wrote to the Thessalonians from Corinth as he would, on a later visit, write to the Romans.

Paul's unhappy experience in Athens caused him to change his approach to preaching in Corinth. According to the Acts of the Apostles, Paul tried to reach the Greek philosophers on their own terms, with high rhetoric and polished argumentation. He was rejected. Thus, he decided to let the Holy Spirit work through his simple and forthright proclamation of the good news without embellishment. He indicated as much when he later wrote to the Corinthians:

> When I came to you, brothers and sisters, I did not come proclaiming the mystery of God to you in lofty words or wisdom. For I decided to know nothing among you except Jesus Christ and him crucified. And I came to you in weakness and in fear and in much trembling. My speech and my proclamation were not with plausible words of wisdom, but with a demonstration of the Spirit and of power (1 Cor 2:1-4).

The City of Corinth

⟨ Corinth was the major city of the Peloponnesian peninsula and the capital of the Roman province of Achaia. It was a flourishing center for almost seven centuries until the Romans destroyed it in 146 B.C.E. on their way to conquering Greece. So strategic was its location, however, that Julius Caesar rebuilt it in 44 B.C.E. and it regained importance by the time of Paul as a commercial center as well as capital of southern Greece. Corinth was over twice the size of Athens, and while Athens turned into a kind of museum for philosophy and literature, Corinth rose in political, economic and intellectual life.

Corinth's importance lay in its location on the isthmus connecting the rest of Greece to the Peloponnesian peninsula. It was on the major road connecting north-south land travel and its twin ports of Cenchreae and Lechaeum connected travel from the Aegean Sea on the east to the Adriatic Sea on the west. Today there is a canal connecting these bodies of water. In Paul's time there was not, but the land was so narrow—only three-and-a-half miles—that small ships could be dragged across the isthmus on wooden logs, or cargo transferred by wagon from one ship across the land to another. This considerably cut stormy sea travel and time around Greece and made Corinth flourish. It is of little surprise that one of the important gods of Corinth was Poseidon, god of the sea. In fact, there was a biannual sports festival in honor of this god. It could well be that Paul was in the city for the Isthmian games in the year 51, and drew a metaphor from the victors who were crowned with a celery wreath: "Do you not know that in a race the runners all compete, but only one receives the prize? ... They do it to receive a perishable wreath, but we an imperishable one" (1 Cor 9:24-25).

Corinth's location gave it all the advantages and disadvantages of a large, urban society. As a new city it was more a Roman colony than Greek, somewhat like Philippi. It had some descendants of former Corinthian exiles, but not much local aristocracy. That afforded the opportunity for many to rise in rank, but also engendered strong competition and flaunting of achieved social status. This commercial center was a magnet for foreigners of every class of society and from every direction: entrepreneurs for trade, and freedpersons and slaves hoping to better their lot by commerce. It was a bustling metropolis and there was money to be made, but not everyone made it. There was a large population of slaves and freedpersons with a feeling of rootlessness and alienation from society. Being on the trade routes, Corinth was subject to the free exchange of thought and culture. There was a theater seating 14,000, a music hall with 3000 seats, any number of temples and shrines, professional clubs for different trades, religious societies and mystery cults. Amidst such pluralism many were easily influenced by new gods and strange ideas. Finally, as a port city Corinth knew all the vices as well as the virtues of sailors on leave. Another important goddess of Corinth was Aphrodite, the goddess of love, with more than a thousand temple slaves dedicated to her as prostitutes. Writers coined the phrases "to act like a Cor-

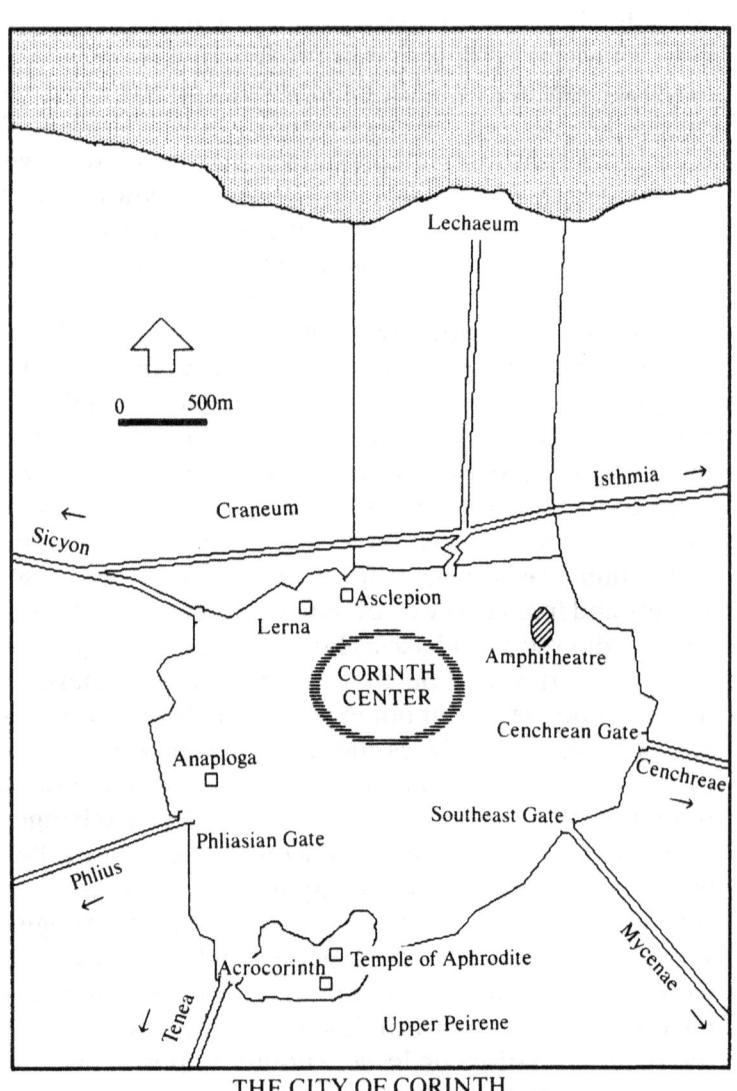

THE CITY OF CORINTH

inthian," meaning to practice fornication, and "Corinthian girl," meaning a prostitute.

In this large cosmopolitan culture there was also a sturdy Jewish community with its own religious influence, its high moral standards, and its strong family life. The Jewish population probably swelled at the time of Paul because the emperor, Claudius, had expelled them from Rome and many came to this haven for refugees. Paul gathered some early converts from this community. We know from the Acts of the Apostles that Crispus, a ruler in the synagogue was baptized, and in a Corinthian letter, Paul mentions Sosthenes who was also a former Jewish leader. In addition there were some Jews who had already become Christians before they were expelled from Rome. Among them were a married couple, Priscilla and Aquila, whom Paul met in Corinth through their mutual trade of tentmaking, and who became coworkers on the mission. Later, in Ephesus, they will convert another Jew named Apollos who will come to Corinth as a famous preacher.

The large part of the Corinthian church was of Gentile background. There were some who were wealthy and who had homes large enough to accommodate the community. The Acts of the Apostles mentions Titius Justus. Paul says he writes Romans from the house of Gaius, who is hosting him and the whole church. In the same letter Paul mentions Erastus, the city treasurer, whose name we also know from a stone inscription found in the theater in Corinth. There were women in prominence as well. Paul speaks of Phoebe, a deacon in the port of Cenchreae. Chloe was apparently a wealthy woman who sent members of her household on business to other cities. Some of her household later brought news of Corinth to Paul in Ephesus. On the whole, however, from what Paul writes, the Corinthian church seems to have gathered many members from the freedpersons and slaves: "Not many of you were wise by human standards, not many were powerful, not many were of noble birth.... God chose what is low and despised in the world" (1 Cor 1:26-28).

All in all, Corinth was a city that needed Paul's message, but problems remained after Paul's first visit. Considering Corinth's character, it is no wonder that most of the problems were not theological, as in the other churches, but more ethical in nature. The letters to the Corinthians were written during the course of what Luke describes as the third missionary journey of Paul. After the apostle completed his first visit, he sailed to Ephesus, left Priscilla and Aquila, and proceeded on to Jerusalem and Antioch. When he undertook his last great missionary journey through Asia Minor and Greece, he returned to Ephesus and stayed over two years. From here came most of the Corinthian letters.

Recent scholarship has determined that Paul wrote more than the two letters and that, indeed, what we now call the second letter to the Corinthians is likely a composite of several different letters written at different times. Deciphering which part of the present texts form which original letters, and reconstructing the historical sequence of correspondence still yield uncertain results. We will follow one possible sequence of events. To begin with, in 1 Corinthians 5:9, Paul mentions a previous letter that spoke of not associating with immoral persons. That letter is now lost or may be in 2 Corinthians 6:14-7:1. This fragment in 2 Corinthians fits poorly where it is presently located in the letter, and speaks about not associating with unbelievers, a topic similar to what Paul indicates as the topic of his earlier letter. Apparently some misunderstood what this meant and reports were brought to

Paul about what they were doing on the basis of their misinterpretation.

Reports to Paul of Problems

Reports of other difficulties were also brought to Paul. While he was in Ephesus, members of Chloe's household brought news of a host of problems that had cropped up in Corinth. Paul wrote what we now call the first letter to the Corinthians in part to address these matters. The problems reported to Paul are dealt with in 1 Corinthians 1-6. To begin with, there was the report of factions within the community. Like so many others who had a chance to change their position in society in Corinth, some Christians felt that they had improved their social status by becoming part of their new community. Then, like so many other Corinthians who were impressed with knowledge and philosophical discussion, they formed schools of thought based on who converted them to Christianity. This led members to become haughty about their new status in a Christian community, which threatened to create factionalism as different groups claimed different leaders and demeaned the others.

Paul describes the factions in Corinth that he heard about: "It has been reported to me by Chloe's people that there are quarrels among you, my brothers and sisters. What I mean is that each of you says, 'I belong to Paul,' or 'I belong to Apollos,' or 'I belong to Cephas,' or 'I belong to Christ'" (1 Cor 1:11). Just what characterized each faction is difficult to say, but we can surmise some general traits based on the leaders proposed as head for each faction. Paul was founder of the church in Corinth and so, it would be natural that many—both Jew and Greek—lined up behind him, but they would also have accepted his approach to Christianity, namely, freedom from all Jewish practices for Gentile Christians, while Jewish Christians would be free to continue with them, if they so desired.

The faction behind Apollos would likely not have differed much in theological perspective, but would have been impressed by the difference in style and presentation between Paul and Apollos. The latter was a Jew from Alexandria in Egypt, trained in the Jewish school of thought that was influenced heavily by the Greek culture. Acts 18:24 says that when Apollos came to Ephesus, "He was an eloquent man, well versed in the scriptures." Apollos would have brought that eloquence into Christianity. In his preaching in Ephesus and then in Corinth, he would have been quite a contrast to Paul's simple and straightforward proclamation. His training in Alexandria would also have led him to more allegorical interpretation of the Old Testament, thus giving him a different way of expounding the truths about Jesus that he shared with Paul.

If, as some scholars deem plausible, Apollos wrote the letter to the Hebrews, we find evidence that he did differ theologically to some degree with Paul. Whereas Paul would have been concerned with freedom from Jewish practices for the Gentiles, Apollos may have advocated elimination of Jewish practices for all Christians. Thus, in terms of the four groups we described earlier as emerging out of the disputes between Antioch and Jerusalem, Paul would have been seen as leader of the more moderate Hellenist/Gentile group and Apollos as representative of the more radical division of that group. In any case, it is likely that Hellenistic Jewish Christians lined up behind Apollos and criticized Paul and those who adhered to Paul's approach.

The faction claiming Peter could have had more serious theological differences with the other groups. They would most likely have been Jewish Christians who either heard Peter himself as a visitor to Corinth or heard representatives from the Jerusalem church claiming to represent Peter. These Christians would have been more favorable toward the perspectives of those whom Acts called the Hebrews in Jerusalem and whom we described earlier as the conservative groups in the debate between Jerusalem and Antioch. While they were probably not the most conservative who demanded circumcision for the Gentile converts, they were, nevertheless, moderately conservative in asking for certain Jewish practices to be performed by these Gentiles as a compromise for harmonious living with Jewish Christians.

There is much debate over whether the statement, "I belong to Christ" represents a fourth faction or is, rather, Paul's refutation of the three preceding factions. If there was a faction that claimed Christ as leader, these were, perhaps, Christians from Jerusalem who had known Jesus in his public life and were claiming superior authority for their community and teaching over the others. While we cannot be certain that they would fit into what we described as the arch-conservative group that emerged out of the Jerusalem-Antioch debate, demanding circumcision even for the Gentiles, they may have been another Jewish Christian group opposed to Paul's teaching about freedom from the law. Another possibility is that this party actually claimed and exaggerated Paul's teaching about being in the risen Christ, and professed a charismatic relationship to Christ in the Spirit, free from any human authority. In any event, this group was citing its life in Christ, not in a healthy Christian way, but in a partisan spirit.

Paul calls all the parties away from petty rivalry and factionalism, reminding them that no one was baptized into anyone except Christ, and that only Christ died for them. He devotes the first four chapters to trying to bring the Corinthians from their self-adulation, as if salvation were based solely on human wisdom or knowledge from a particular teacher. They should rather understand that knowledge is in the service of love and unity, and all comes ultimately from God: "Let the one who boasts, boast in the Lord. . . . When one says, 'I belong to Paul,' and another, 'I belong to Apollos,' are you not merely human? . . . I planted, Apollos watered, but God gave the growth" (1 Cor 1:31; 3:4, 6). The overconfidence in knowledge and the problem of factionalism will show themselves in other ways and will be a continuing problem in Corinth, as we shall see later in this chapter and in the next.

Another major problem in the Corinthian church seems to have been misunderstanding of Paul's preaching about freedom from the law. Some of this was combined with misunderstanding about the material world and its implications for human sexuality. It seems that for a number of the Christians, the influence of philosophy and the pleasures of a port city worked strange combinations. These Christians brought over their negative view of the material world and envisioned salvation as a purely spiritual matter. But they then drew the conclusion that, if Christ is saving only one's soul, it does not matter what one does with the body. Thus, there was sexual scandal in the community. One man was living with his stepmother (1 Cor 5) and others were going to prostitutes (1 Cor 6:12-20). They were saying sex doesn't matter. They were likewise misinterpreting Paul's principles to support their view, saying that even Paul claimed, "All things are lawful to me."

These happenings were also part of the report brought by Chloe's household. Paul challenges the church, telling the community to ostracize the immoral man in order to bring him to his senses (1 Cor 5:4-5), and clarifying what he means by freedom. Christ saves the whole person, body and soul. It does matter what one does with human sexuality and the material world. Likewise, freedom is from the law as the central or the external authority, but is not permission for licentiousness. "'All things are lawful for me,' but not all things are beneficial. . . . Do you not know that your body is a temple of the Holy Spirit within you?" (1 Cor 6:12, 19). In this section Paul also clarifies that this is what he meant in his first letter about shunning immoral persons, namely, not a withdrawal from the world or from daily human existence, but avoidance of those who give scandal within the Christian community (1 Cor 5:9-13).

One final report that Paul receives from Chloe's merchants is that there is scandal arising from Christians "doing their laundry in public" by bringing lawsuits against each other in the secular courts. Paul writes back advice: "Can it be that there is no one among you wise enough to decide between one believer and another, but a believer goes to court against a believer—and before unbelievers at that? In fact, to have lawsuits at all with one another is already a defeat for you. Why not rather be wronged?" (1 Cor 6:5-7).

Topics from the Corinthians' Letter

Besides the oral reports that they brought, it seems that Chloe's household also brought a letter with questions from Corinth about several matters. They all revolved around misinterpretations of Paul's earlier teaching, and the apostle devotes the rest of 1 Corinthians, from chapter 7, to answering these questions. One problem was another form of the same mistaken view of salvation as a purely spiritual matter, only this view concluded to a rigorous sexual asceticism rather than libertinism. Some of the community were claiming that if Christ is risen, then we are all in his new life and sexual differences are eliminated. It also means that one is to withdraw from material reality as much as possible and that, therefore, sexual relations are to be avoided. Marriages are to be dissolved and prohibited. The letter brought a statement from the Corinthians which they no doubt wanted Paul to comment on: "It is well for a man not to touch a woman" (1 Cor 7:1).

Paul had to refute this opposite distortion of his preaching about salvation in the risen Christ. He had to reaffirm once again that Christ saves the whole person and that human sexuality can be a blessed part of Christian existence. It must be admitted that Paul does not indicate the highest motives and the deepest dimensions of marriage, but he intends at this time merely to offer the minimum reasons why it is foolish to say that one should not marry. His argument is similar to that of the Stoics, as if to say that the Corinthians already had basic reasons for marriage even before their conversion and should not lose sight of those reasons afterward: "Because of cases of sexual immorality, each man should have his own wife and each woman her own husband" (1 Cor 7:2); "To the unmarried and the widows I say that it is well for them to remain unmarried as I am. But if they are not practicing self-control, they should marry. For it is better to marry than to be aflame with passion" (1 Cor 7:8-9). One will have to wait for another time for the full development of the theology of marriage. Paul will even agree with his erroneous community that celibacy is a possibility (1 Cor

7:25-35), but it is not for all and it is not imposed. Paul will at least maintain the place of marriage and will even go so far as to insist on the equality of man and woman in that relation: "The wife does not have authority over her own body, but the husband does; likewise the husband does not have authority over his own body, but the wife does" (1 Cor 7:4).

The Corinthians' placement of great value in knowledge bred another problem about which they wrote. They knew that idols were empty, so that meat which had been used in pagan sacrifice and then sold at a good price in the public markets was no threat. Christians could buy and eat it. They flaunted a saying which they probably wrote in their letter to Paul: "All of us possess knowledge" (1 Cor 8:1). The implication for them was that anyone scandalized by this is ignorant. They also again misused Paul's principle to further their argument: "All things are lawful" (1 Cor 10:23). Paul straightens out their misunderstandings in his reply in 1 Corinthians 8-10: "Knowledge puffs up, but love builds up.... If food is a cause of their falling, I will never eat meat, so that I may not cause one of them to fall" (8:1, 13); "'All things are lawful,' but not all things are beneficial.... If someone says to you, 'This has been offered in sacrifice,' then do not eat it, out of consideration for the one who informed you, and for the sake of conscience—I mean the other's conscience, not your own." (10:23, 28-29).

Misunderstanding of the role of human sexuality and the material world within Christianity probably underlies the famous debate about women covering their heads in worship. The Corinthians appear to have reasoned as follows: If we are all one in the risen Christ, then not only should there be equality between the sexes, but sexual differences ought to be wiped out. Let the women abandon feminine dress and preach in worship with head uncovered. Paul sought to maintain equality of the sexes without denying differences. The veil represented feminine dress and differentiation for him, and so he marshalled arguments from Genesis and creation to maintain the veil: "Any woman who prays or prophesies with her head unveiled disgraces her head—it is one and the same thing as having her head shaved. . . . For a man ought not to have his head veiled, since he is the image and reflection of God; but woman is the reflection of man" (1 Cor 11:5, 7). The custom of the veil seems quaint to us and the arguments not compelling. Even Paul knew his arguments were weak and finally based his argument on the fact that it simply was not the custom in the churches (11:16). At any rate, his point about sexual differences was valid, even if the way he wanted to enforce it no longer makes sense, and we must also note that he did agree that women as well as men should preach in the assembly of worship.

Thinking that life in the risen Christ was to remove one from the material world led to other problems finally discussed in 1 Corinthians 12-15. It led some to see the charism of speaking in tongues as the most important gift, showing that one has the Spirit of the risen Christ. This is so because in their view the gift of tongues brought one as close as possible to an out-of-body experience. Paul would admit that tongues could be a manifestation of the Spirit, but it was not essential, not the most important, and not to dominate the worship. He placed tongues last on his list of the gifts of the Spirit (12:10), said that all gifts should be in the service of love (13:1-13), said that intelligible prophecy was more important (14:5), and ordered that tongues be limited and controlled in worship (14:27). In this section, a passage also tells women to be silent in the churches, but since it contradicts the earlier statements of

Paul about women preaching, it intends either particular women or silence from the particular kind of speaking in tongues, or it is a later insertion from a church moving away from Paul's principle of equality. Finally, demeaning of material reality led some to deny even that Jesus really had a bodily resurrection, or that they would. Paul spoke to that problem in 1 Corinthians 15, and verse 20 makes both points crisply: "Christ has been raised from the dead, the first fruits of those who have died."

If 1 Corinthians 16:10 gives any indication, Paul sent this letter and then followed it with a visit from Timothy. He also sent greetings from Priscilla and Aquila who were in Ephesus with him (16:19), and from Apollos who apparently had returned from Corinth to Ephesus (16:12). Paul continues to speak affectionately of Apollos, indicating that his quarrel was less with Apollos than with the faction that stood under the name. In any case, the problems in Corinth were not finally resolved by 1 Corinthians and a series of events and letters followed. These will be the topic of our next chapter.

Continued Corinthian Correspondence

Paul's attempts to answer the questions and to solve the problems of the Corinthian church seem not to have been achieved with the letter we call 1 Corinthians. His subsequent writings show that he had to follow his letter with a visit directly from Ephesus to Corinth to try to resolve crises (2 Cor 2:1; 13:1). Even then, he was unsuccessful, returned to Ephesus and wrote what he later called a "letter of tears" to Corinth (2 Cor 2:4). This seems to be contained now in 2 Corinthians 10-13, which has the elements of a strong letter addressing unresolved problems. Then he dispatched Titus and went himself to Macedonia to be comforted by his friends there (2 Cor 2:12-14). Titus returned with good news that the crises were resolved (2 Cor 7:6). Paul wrote a letter of reconciliation and eventually also appealed for money for the poor in Jerusalem. We have this correspondence in 2 Corinthians 1-9. Paul made one final visit from Macedonia to Corinth. In this chapter we will use the above scenario to provide the social background and a sketch of the continuing correspondence between Paul and his troubled church after the writing of 1 Corinthians.

Increased Opposition in Corinth

We are not sure whether the Corinthian community persisted in the same problems addressed in 1 Corinthians, or whether new problems arose. In either case, the difficulties gave rise to bitter opposition between Paul and a certain segment of the Corinthian community, so that Paul's very authority was impugned. The struggle led Paul to define and describe his role as apostle. Thus, in the later Corinthian correspondence, which we now have as 2 Corinthians, we have the most personal writing of Paul and his most intimate thoughts about his work and his relationship with the churches which he founded. Let us look more closely now in 2 Corinthians, not only at the problems which persisted, but also at the meaning of ministry as exemplified personally by Paul.

First of all, what were the problems that continued within the Corinthian community? We do not know exactly. Any information we have on the problems—as also on the original problems addressed in 1 Corinthians—is reconstructed from the solutions that Paul offers in his letters. Paul did not state what exactly were the problems or even whether they were the same ones which he had addressed in his earlier correspondence. What is clear is that these problems had taken a personal turn. After writing 1 Corinthians from Ephesus, Paul heard of continuing difficulties, so he dropped everything to make a direct visit to that troubled community. Apparently resistance hardened, and a group of Corinthians attacked Paul personally, challenging his very authority as an apostle. In fact, one member publicly defied Paul.

Were the opponents a carryover from the factions that Paul challenged in his first letter, some still saying, "I am of Peter" while others proclaimed, "I am of Paul"? There

A POSSIBLE CHRONOLOGY FOR THE CORINTHIAN CORRESPONDENCE

1) Paul writes a letter prior to 1 Corinthians (cf 1 Cor 5:9) from Ephesus to Corinth, now lost or perhaps partially preserved in 2 Corinthians 6:14-7:1.
2) Rumors, oral reports and a letter from Corinth to Paul all reveal continuing problems and cause Paul to write what is now 1 Corinthians.
3) Paul tells the Corinthians that he plans to spend the winter with them after passing through Macedonia (1 Cor 16:5-6).
4) Paul follows up the sending of 1 Corinthians with a visit to Corinth by Timothy (1 Cor 16:10).
5) Problems persist, forcing Paul to change his plans and to visit Corinth directly from Ephesus to try to resolve the crisis (cf 2 Cor 2:1).
6) Paul is unsuccessful in Corinth, leaves the city, and from Ephesus writes a "letter of tears" (cf 2 Cor 2:4; 7:8). This letter may be lost or may be preserved as 2 Corinthians 10-13.
7) Paul thus revises travel plans, hoping to visit Macedonia after going to Corinth and then to return to Corinth for the winter (2 Cor 1:15-16).
8) Circumstances apparently force another change in plans. Besides having to confront the persisting problems in Corinth, Paul also has to defend himself against charges of vacillating, because of his frequent changing of travel plans (2 Cor 1:17-23).
9) Paul seems to send the letter of tears with Titus (2 Cor 7:6). Paul himself travels to Macedonia, while still awaiting word from Titus (2 Cor 2:12-13).
10) Titus catches up with Paul in Macedonia with good news that the problems have been resolved in Corinth (2 Cor 7:6). Paul writes a letter of reconciliation and resumes his project of taking up a collection for the poor. This correspondence seems preserved in 2 Corinthians 1-9.
11) Titus seems to return to Corinth to coordinate the work of the collection (2 Cor 8:6, 16-17). Paul himself makes a final visit to Corinth from Macedonia to receive the collection for the poor in Jerusalem (2 Cor 8:3-5).

seems a good possibility that at least the Peter faction was still strong, though, as we pointed out earlier, it is not clear that Peter was personally behind it. A group of Christians from Jewish background may have been asserting their views about Christianity and were citing Peter and the Jerusalem church as authorities against Paul and the Gentiles. Paul had already written about all being baptized into the one body of Christ, but apparently the disputes would not dissolve. In fact, they seem to have worsened. It appears that Christian outsiders came into Corinth pushing their Jewish-Christian views and challenging Paul's apostolic authority. Paul refers to them sarcastically as superlative apostles: "I was not at all inferior to these super-apostles, even though I am nothing. The signs of a true apostle were performed among you with utmost patience, signs and wonders and mighty works" (2 Cor 12:11-12).

These superlative apostles raised objections that forced Paul to give intimate reflections on his apostolic ministry. He did this first in the letter of tears and then followed up that teaching with further observations in his letter of reconciliation. We will look at each of these in turn. From Paul's responses we can surmise what the opponents were saying and thus what determined Paul's statements. Beginning with the letter of tears, we notice that most of the arguments of the opponents were personal, *ad hominem* arguments against Paul. One of them tried to cut Paul down to size and make him vulnerable to attack by impugning his preaching abilities, probably asking the community why it would be cowed into listening to Paul's views when he was so unskilled in speaking. They said: "His letters are weighty and strong, but his bodily presence is weak, and his speech contemptible" (2 Cor 10:10).

This claim of the opponents may actually contain some truth about Paul's preaching. It may indicate something that we would not expect or envision, namely, that Paul may have been only an ordinary speaker and not the great rhetorician that imagination often makes him out to be. It is interesting, in any case, that Paul does not refute their criticism directly, but says that it is off the point. He writes: "I think that I am not in the least inferior to these super-apostles. I may be untrained in speech, but not in knowledge" (2 Cor 11:5-6). True ministry centers on the *message* about the risen Lord, not just on the rhetorical skills or other *means* used to proclaim the message. For Paul the rationale, the focus and the joy of his apostolate is Jesus Christ as Lord.

Later, in the letter of reconciliation, Paul will develop a related point more fully. For his opponents who exalt their Jewish credentials and, perhaps, their link with the Jewish Jesus and the Jerusalem church, Paul argues that, while Jewish revelation is indeed God's gift and not to be spurned, it is, nevertheless, not the final gift for Christians. Everyone seeks to know the reality of God as God truly is. From a Christian perspective, the old covenant shows that reality partially, while the new covenant in Christ brings full clarity. As Paul puts it, everyone is trying to see the radiant glory of God, but, "To this very day whenever Moses is read, a veil lies over their minds, but when one turns to the Lord, the veil is removed" (2 Cor 3:15-16).

Paul's View of Ministry

It is this clear vision that establishes Paul's role as an apostle and lays the foundation for what he sees as ministry in Corinth and in the churches. Paul continues to write:

"We do not proclaim ourselves, we proclaim Jesus Christ as Lord and ourselves as your slaves for Jesus' sake. For it is the God who said, 'Let light shine out of darkness,' who has shone in our hearts to give the light of the knowledge of the glory of God in the face of Jesus Christ" (2 Cor 4:5-6). Paul admits that this light is in a frail human being and that ministry is not without its setbacks and failures. He says: "We have this treasure in clay jars, so that it may be made clear that this extraordinary power belongs to God and does not come from us" (2 Cor 4:7). This point in the letter of reconciliation picks up a point already made in the letter of tears, precipitated by another accusation of the opponents.

These adversaries were boasting of their legitimacy as the true apostles to Corinth, not only because of their Jewish heritage, but also because of their dedication to their ministry in trial and suffering. Paul countered that they had no advantage over him. He was reluctant to boast of his own credentials, but he thought himself better than his opponents in these qualifications:

> Whatever anyone dares to boast of—I am speaking as a fool—I also dare to boast of that. Are they Hebrews? So am I. Are they Israelites? So am I. Are they descendants of Abraham? So am I. Are they ministers of Christ? I am talking like a madman—I am a better one: with far greater labors, far more imprisonments, with countless floggings, and often near death (2 Cor 11:21-23).

In validating the authenticity of his ministry Paul also established another trait of his apostolic mission. It was a somewhat ironic trait. Instead of experiencing dramatic success, personal glory and world acclaim, Paul knew failure, sickness and other suffering, including the turmoil in Corinth itself. But for him this was inherent in authentic ministry. Paul never considered himself more the preacher of Christ than when he showed in his very life the cross as the way to resurrection. That is why he was not impressed by the haughty claims of the superlative apostles. Rather, he put himself forward as the true servant of Christ, being weak with the weak, bearing a "thorn in the flesh" (2 Cor 12:7), and boasting in his weakness that the power of Christ might be manifest in him and through him.

Apparently there were still some lingering criticisms of Paul's authority, even as the problems were clearing up in Corinth, so Paul stressed one or two further traits of his ministry even in the letter of reconciliation. One of the continuing criticisms was that Paul was fickle. He had changed plans for his visits to Corinth several times during this crisis. Originally, he had planned to pass through Macedonia and to visit Corinth for a winter (1 Cor 16:5). That plan changed when Paul made the extra visit directly to Corinth, probably after Timothy returned to say that 1 Corinthians was unsuccessful in its results. Apparently after that visit and Paul's return to Ephesus, he next intended to go back directly to Corinth, then to travel to Macedonia and finally to return to Corinth before going to Jerusalem (2 Cor 1:15-16). This, too, changed, because Paul did not go immediately back to Corinth, leaving Ephesus instead for Macedonia before finally passing through Corinth (2 Cor 2:12-13).

With all the changes, the Corinthian adversaries said that Paul simply could not make up his mind and was not to be relied on. Paul gave reasons for his frequent change of plans and asserted that the focus of his ministry remained constant and centered on his bond with the community in love and in the risen Christ:

As surely as God is faithful, our word to you has not been "Yes and No." For the Son of God, Jesus Christ, whom we proclaimed among you, Silvanus and Timothy and I, was not "Yes and No"; but in him it is always "Yes." For in him every one of God's promises is a "Yes.". . . . It is God who establishes us with you in Christ and has anointed us. . . . I call on God as witness against me: it was to spare you that I did not come again to Corinth. I do not mean to imply that we lord it over your faith; rather we are workers with you for your joy, for you stand firm in the faith. So I made up my mind not to make you another painful visit. . . . I wrote you out of much distress and anguish of heart and with many tears, not to cause you pain, but to let you know the abundant love that I have for you (2 Cor 1:18-2:4).

Another criticism from the opponents was that Paul had never met Jesus in history, whereas they had, and they built their views on those who were the original disciples of Jesus. Paul responded; "From now on, therefore, we regard no one from a human point of view; even though we once knew Christ from a human point of view, we know him no longer in that way" (2 Cor 5:16). Paul means that his preaching is based not primarily on a Jesus who lived in the past and is seen from a purely human, historical point of view, but on a risen Christ who lives always in the present and is seen from a faith perspective. It is not clear from this statement that Paul did not know Jesus in history before the resurrection, but many scholars take it that way. In any case, even if he did, such experience was not important as the basis for Paul's apostolic ministry. Paul already said this, in effect, when he stated in 1 Corinthians that what makes him an apostle just as much as Peter and the others is that he has seen the risen Christ (1 Cor 9:1).

One further objection was over Paul's credentials. The

opponents claimed that they bore letters of recommendation from the Jewish-Christian community which gave them authority to preach in the churches. Paul responded; "Surely we do not need, as some do, letters of recommendation to you or from you, do we? You yourselves are our letter, written on our hearts, ... a letter of Christ, prepared by us, written not with ink but with the Spirit of the living God" (2 Cor 3:1-3). The sign of authentic ministry is not primarily from external documents or designation, but from the experience of the risen Lord communicated from one to another.

Ultimately, the goal of Paul's apostolic ministry was to bring all into the unity of the body of Christ. In concrete terms for Paul, that meant that his suffering at the hands of the Corinthians was to be itself a patient witness to lead to reconciliation in the risen Christ. Throughout all the conflict Paul kept his love for that church. He even called for reconciliation with that person who had publicly affronted him on his painful visit (2 Cor 2:5-11; 7:8-13). Finally, Paul summed up his entire ministry as one of reconciliation: "If anyone is in Christ, there is a new creation. . . . All this is from God, who reconciled us to himself through Christ, and has given us the ministry of reconciliation. . . . So we are ambassadors for Christ, since God is making his appeal through us. . . . Be reconciled to God" (2 Cor 5:17-20).

The Collection for Jerusalem

One final conflict which is indicated in the letter of tears and is discussed still in the later correspondence revolved around financial matters. His foes resented pressures from Paul for a collection for the poor in Jerusalem. They combined this with skepticism over why Paul worked as a tentmaker and refused their support in his ministry among them. Whether as a ruse to undermine his authority or as a sincere conviction on their part, it seems that they claimed that Paul was really conniving to make money off of them, pretending not to want any stipend, but skimming funds for himself from the collection. As Paul wrote to these adversaries; "[You say] since I was crafty, I took you in by deceit" (2 Cor 12:16).

This conflict may actually have had deeper roots in the economic factions that Paul had to challenge in 1 Corinthians 11:17-34. The wealthy in the Christian community were prejudiced toward the poor and were avoiding them. According to 1 Corinthians, these divisions were manifest at the eucharistic celebrations in Corinth. In those days the Eucharist culminated an actual dinner together in one of the larger households that could accommodate thirty to fifty Christians. The dinners, however, were far from edifying. Obviously, not everyone could fit into the formal dining area and some had to eat in the inner courtyard around which the house was designed. However, hosts apparently divided the groups according to social status, inviting the wealthier guests into the dining area and requiring the poorer members to sit around the courtyard. To make matters worse, it seems that better food was reserved for those in the dining area and, since they had the leisure to spend more time away from work, they often started before poorer servants could attend.

Paul wrote in 1 Corinthians about the irony of such a situation. After all of this discrimination and prejudice, the guests then gathered to celebrate their unity in the body of Christ in the eucharist. They were celebrating a lie. Paul counselled them to discern the true nature of the body of Christ and to strive to achieve it. The wealthy had to care for the poor. They should wait for each other before eating

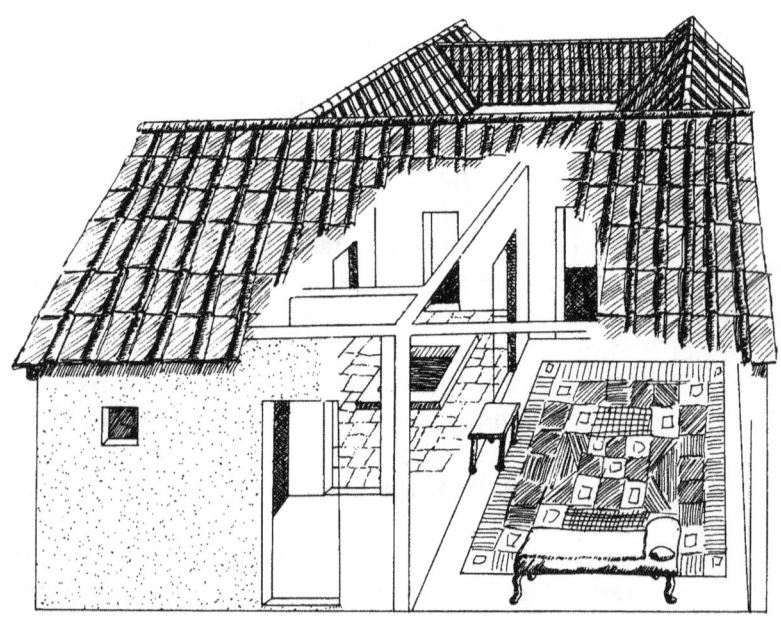

A diagram of a house in Paul's time, similar to the ones that served as household churches and provided the places for celebration of the Eucharist.

dinner and there should not be some hungry and others drunk. In other words, the eucharist is a meal to promote unity in Christ and it will be meaningful only insofar as Christians strive toward that unity through mutual concern. This includes concern for the economic and social issues of the time.

Apparently the better-off Christians in Corinth were still somewhat apathetic toward their obligations to the poor and it showed itself in resentment over the collection. Paul first had to defend himself against accusations of embezzling money: "Did I take advantage of you through any of those whom I sent to you? I urged Titus to go, and sent the brother with him. Titus did not take advantage of you, did he? Did we not conduct ourselves with the same spirit? Did we not take the same steps?" (2 Cor 12:17-18). Then Paul had to attack the deeper problem of apathy toward the poor and the feeling of resentment at being pressured to help. While he would not take money for himself, he saw it as an obligation in the body of Christ to raise money for the poor:

> [I am not seeking contributions] as a command, but I am testing the genuineness of your love against the earnestness of others. For you know the generous act of our Lord Jesus Christ, that though he was rich, yet for your sakes he became poor, so that by his poverty you might become rich. . . . I do not mean that there should be relief for others and pressure on you, but it is a question of a fair balance between your present abundance and their need, so that their abundance may be for your need, in order that there may be a fair balance (2 Cor 8:8-14).

The collection for the poor remained a major concern for Paul even after reconciliation with Corinth. He speaks about it in two entire chapters of the letter of reconciliation. Some scholars believe that 2 Corinthians 8 and 9 are parts of additional letters written after the letter of reconciliation, which would have been 2 Corinthians 1-7, rather than chapters 1-9. In either case Titus, who was initially responsible for organizing this collection among the churches in Greece, was sent back to Corinth: "We might urge Titus that, as he had already made a beginning, so he should also complete this generous undertaking among you" (2 Cor 8:6).

In the long run, Paul had a deeper purpose in resolving these issues. He hoped to promote the reconciliation and the unity between Christians of Gentile and Jewish backgrounds, thus solving the greater problems that had begun with the church in Antioch, as we described in a previous chapter. In getting the wealthy in Gentile Corinth and elsewhere to help the poor in Jewish Jerusalem, he hoped to help the Gentiles see their links to the Jewish heritage that preceded them. At the same time, in getting Jerusalem to accept the collection from the Gentile churches, he hoped to have Jewish Christians recognize the legitimacy of Gentile Christianity and thus remove the basis for opposition from people like the superlative apostles in Corinth. In the end Paul was successful in solving the crises in Corinth, exercising his apostolic ministry as he described it, as a servant of Christ, an earthen vessel, a minister of reconciliation.

The Church in Galatia

Like the church in Corinth, the church in Galatia challenged Paul with serious problems. Before treating that theological debate, we must consider the social world of the Galatians. Unlike the other recipients of Paul's letters, Galatia was not a single city, but a region in central Anatolia, the ancient name for Turkey. Its location is uncertain, because the name Galatia came to be applied to different territories in that general area.

The Territory of Galatia

Originally, Galatia designated an area on the central plateau around present-day Ankara, settled by Gauls or Celts—curiously enough the same ethnic group that also migrated to what is now France, Ireland and other parts of western Europe. By the time of Paul, however, the Romans had used the name for a legal jurisdiction or province that included the original Gallic or Celtic territory but also extended farther south to include cities like Iconium, Lystra and Derbe. Scholars still debate whether Paul is addressing the original ethnic territory of the Celts or the wider legal territory of the Romans. The principal reason for thinking that Paul is writing to the wider Roman prov-

A map of North and South Galatia, showing the original northern ethnic territory and the later Roman province which encompassed the south as well.

ince is that the Acts of the Apostles has stories about Paul visiting the cities of Iconium, Lystra and Derbe, while it has no stories about his visiting the more northern territory.

Still, it is interesting to note that even Luke, in the Acts of the Apostles, does not refer to these southern cities as Galatia. In addition, while Acts has no particular stories about the more northern area, it does mention twice that Paul visited the area of Phrygia and Galatia (16:6; 18:23). A further support of the so-called northern theory is that in popular parlance at that time the name Galatia referred to the ethnic region and not the Roman legal territory. Finally, the content of the letter seems better to support a northern community. For example, since the letter deals with freedom from the Jewish law, some have suggested that this would indicate the southern region where there was a large Jewish population. On the contrary, it makes better sense that the people addressed were a population recently infatuated with Jewish practices under the influence of visiting Christian missionaries with Jewish background. We will presume, therefore, that Paul wrote his letter to the central area of Anatolia.

Because of the uncertainty over location there is also debate over just when Paul would have written the letter to the Galatians. If Galatia included the more southern cities such as Iconium, Lystra and Derbe, then Paul could have written his letter quite early in his career, perhaps as he was beginning his journeys to Greece. If, as we presume, Galatia refers to the northern area, then Paul would have probably written the letter after he reached Ephesus or Macedonia at the start of his last journey through western Turkey and Greece.

The fact that Paul addresses his letter to a general region probably indicates that his ministry there was to little towns and not to any particular cities. This would be in keeping with the nature of the area, which was rugged terrain, hard to farm, cold in winter, and inhabited by tribes with an ancestry that went back long before the Romans. In fact, Romans were not numerous in this region, living in the few cities and considering themselves a civilizing influence on the native population. Prominent in this region, as throughout Asia Minor, was the worship of the Great Earth Mother, known often as Cybele, but also bearing the names of local fertility goddesses. Paul probably had in mind such pagan practices when he warned the Galatians not to revert to their former practices: "Formerly, when you did not know God, you were enslaved to beings that by nature are not gods. Now, however, that you have come to know God, or rather to be known by God, how can you turn back again to the weak and beggarly elemental spirits? How can you want to be enslaved to them again? You are observing special days, and months, and seasons, and years" (4:8-10).

It seems likely that in speaking about days and seasons Paul, besides criticizing a return to idolatry, is also referring to another problem that arose in Galatia only after he had left—the entrance of Jewish Christians who were convincing the Gentile Christian converts of the necessity to adopt Jewish practices as essential to their faith. This caught Paul by surprise and was changing his relationship to the Galatian church. Up to that point these Galatians were intimate friends of Paul, showing affection as deep as that which the Philippians showed the apostle. In fact, Paul stayed in that region because of some severe illness, and the Galatians not only heard his message but took precious care of him. "You know that it was because of a physical infirmity that I first announced the gospel to you. Though my condition put you to the test, you did not scorn or despise me, but welcomed me as an angel of God, as

Christ Jesus. . . . Had it been possible, you would have torn out your eyes and given them to me" (4:13-15).

Because of the reference to the eyes, some scholars have guessed that Paul had an eye ailment, but of course, his description could be purely figurative. In any case the affection of the Galatians and their adherence to Paul was clear. But then, it seems, some troublemakers came to Galatia, as they did to Corinth, and turned the community against Paul, questioning his very authority. We do not know how Paul heard about the new problem, but the tone of his letter to the Galatians shows that he was certainly perplexed about them, somewhat upset and perhaps even a bit angry, though he does still call them his little children with whom he is in labor again to form Christ in them (4:19). Paul's dismay is clear from the fact that he omits the customary thanksgiving at the start of his letter and says right after the greeting that he is astonished that the Galatians are deserting him.

Paul wastes no time in addressing his conflicts with this community. His letter has three major foci: the first two chapters concentrate on history, the next two on theology and the final two on the ethical consequences of his teaching. Of course, such divisions are not ironclad, and the topics overlap. Nevertheless, these divisions will help our study. Paul begins with historical information because he is trying to verify his apostolic authority. No doubt, the Galatian missionaries were boasting of true authority based on the Jerusalem community and were impugning Paul's as not being based on the center of Jewish Christianity. So, Paul affirms that his authority derives from the fact that he has seen the risen Lord, thereby receiving his call directly from God and not from other human beings, not even from the other apostles in Jerusalem. "When God . . . was pleased to reveal his Son to me, so that I might proclaim him among the Gentiles, I did not confer with any human being, nor did I go up to Jerusalem to those who were already apostles before me" (1:16-17).

Paul began to preach immediately as a way of showing no need to get anyone's permission to be an apostle. Three years after his conversion Paul did go to Jerusalem, but only for a short private meeting with Peter and James, and certainly not to have them confer authority on him. After this meeting Paul began his missionary journeys. The eventual entrance of Gentiles into the church and the conflicts that arose between Christians of Jewish and of Gentile background led Paul to Jerusalem once again. "After fourteen years I went up again to Jerusalem with Barnabas, taking Titus along with me.... I laid before them... the gospel that I proclaim among the Gentiles, in order to make sure that I was not running, or had not run, in vain" (2:1-2).

Paul was afraid that his work would be ruined and he would have run in vain, if Jewish Christians imposed circumcision and other Jewish practices on Gentile converts. He said that Peter, James and John agreed with him that no practices should be imposed and that Paul should continue his work among the Gentiles. They asked further only that Paul take up a collection for the poor in Jerusalem. Later on, Peter visited Antioch and, under pressure from disciples of James, reneged on his agreement not to impose Jewish practices on the Gentiles. Peter left the table when disciples of James were shocked that Peter was eating non-kosher food with Gentiles. Paul says he opposed Peter to his face for not standing by his principles.

Theology and Ethics in Galatians

His brief run through history not only affirmed Paul's authority as an apostle in his own right, but also declared his message as the true gospel over against what the Judaizers, the Jewish-Christian intruders, were telling the Galatians. Paul develops that gospel in more detail in chapters three and four of his letter, focusing on theology. Here the main point is that all Christians are made just and saved from sin, not by their own works in keeping the Jewish law, but by God's grace in Christ received through faith. Much of Paul's argumentation in this section seems based on what his opponents were saying and in how they were using the Old Testament to buttress their points. Paul tries to stand their arguments on their head, using the same biblical texts to turn the arguments against them. We can reconstruct the main lines of their arguments and Paul's refutation.

The Judaizers saw their birth as Jews something that separated them from the Gentiles, whom they saw as sinners. It also gave them the law as the means for attaining salvation. They based their arguments on the story of Abraham who was promised blessing if he left his tribal gods to believe in and worship the one true God. The covenant and promises to Abraham were expanded to include an entire nation through Moses, and Abraham's faith and worship was carried on through the law given by Moses. True righteousness, therefore, came from being part of the line of Abraham, either by physical birth or by conversion that included circumcision. Belonging to Abraham entailed keeping the law in all things, and this obligation was expressed in Deuteronomy by saying that one who did not follow the law in all things was cursed. Since the promise and the law came from God, those who follow Christ still receive the promise by following the law.

Paul speaks from his own experience as well as that of the Galatians to turn the arguments around. He points out that the problem with Jewish law is that no one can ultimately keep all of its prescriptions. While the law was God's gift to show us how to behave, it could not actually effect better behavior. Sin wound up getting the upper hand and we broke the law. This does not mean that the law was against the promises or was not God's gift. It means only that the law was inadequate and that God had a better gift in mind. Thus, the law was a temporary custodian, doing its best to keep us out of sin, but eventually having to yield to Jesus who could touch us by his own graced presence and could transform our sinful natures. (See Galatians 3:19-26.)

Besides his imagery about the law as a custodian, Paul makes his point by reversing other arguments from scripture. In doing so, he uses a typically rabbinic method. He takes Old Testament texts and rereads them to show how they are speaking about contemporary situations. First he argues from the law itself that the law cannot save. He says: "All who rely on the works of the law are under a curse; for it is written, 'Cursed is everyone who does not observe and obey all the things written in the book of the law'" (3:10). Paul reads the text to mean, not that one must keep the law in all things, but that the law cannot save. The law requires that every command be kept or it must curse the sinner. Now none of us can keep every command of the law, so we are cursed instead of saved by law.

Another Old Testament text says, "He who through faith is righteous shall live," so Paul draws on it to show that we are saved through faith in what God can do in us through Jesus, not through faith which tries to keep the law. This, of course, is Paul's new interpretation of what the text means by the word "faith." A third text says, "Cursed be everyone who hangs on a tree." Paul applies it to Christ as a way of saying that Christ on the tree of the cross, in being cursed by the law, absorbed all curses and thereby freed us from the law. Finally, Paul puts the three points together to say, "Christ redeemed us from the curse of the law by becoming a curse for us, [hanging from the tree of the cross,] . . . so that we might receive the promise of the Spirit through faith" (3:13-14).

We might rephrase, as follows, Paul's theology of freedom from the law and of redemption: The law shows its powerlessness and our predicament by ultimately being able to do no more than declare us guilty of sin. (It curses us.) Christ takes on our human existence and lives a life without sin. At the same time, however, he experiences all the effects of sin around him, including the hostility and alienation from others, and the ignominy of death even on a cross. (He becomes a curse for us, hanging on a tree.) Yet he never succumbs to sin and by his resurrection he definitively conquers sin and its consequences. (He absorbs all the curse of the law and exhausts it.) Moreover, by sharing his life with us through the Spirit received in faith, he enables us finally to avoid sin, which the law was never able to help us do. (He redeems us from the curse of the law by giving us the promise of the Spirit.)

Paul rereads the story of Abraham and his two sons to make a further argument from scripture about salvation through faith. The opponents were citing Abraham's son, Isaac, as the true seed of Abraham who exemplifies the reception of circumcision and the keeping of Jewish practices to be saved. They equated the Jews and the Jewish Christians with Isaac. By a combination of Old Testament texts Paul interprets the story to show the opposite. According to Paul, the Jews and those who retain Jewish practices are represented by Ishmael, the other son, and are thus presented as slaves to the law; the other son, Isaac, represents Christians free from law as heirs to the promises of salvation that come from life in the Spirit.

Having made his point about where true salvation comes from, Paul does not thereby intend freedom from the law to mean lawlessness or licentiousness. Thus, he devotes the last two chapters of his letter to ethical considerations. Freedom should be understood more as "freedom for," i.e., commitment to what is genuinely salvific, rather than simply "freedom from," i.e., simply the absence of any commitment at all. To be free from the law means that the law is superseded and no longer central as the means of salvation. It does not imply that the law is wrong or meaningless in what it requires. Jewish Christians can still follow the good things that the law requires, but indeed even they are able to do so, not because of the law, but because the Spirit enables them. Gentile Christians should not be subjected to the law as such, but should be moved by the Spirit to live in the same moral way that the law intended. Nevertheless, they will do it whether there is Jewish law or not.

Thus, all are free *from* the law as essential, but free *for* achieving what the law intended in the first place, but was powerless to really bring about. So, Paul speaks of obligation that accompanies true freedom and talks about living according to the genuine intentions of the Jewish law even while we are free from it. "You were called to freedom, brothers and sisters; only do not use your freedom as an opportunity for self-indulgence, but through love become slaves to one another. For the whole law is summed up in a single commandment, 'You shall love your neighbor as yourself'" (Gal 5:13-14).

In the long run, history, theology and ethics combine to encourage the Galatians to live as a community in the Spirit and no longer under their pagan ways or under the imposition of laws that are not the real and effective means of salvation. Paul's authentic gospel, his teaching about freedom from the law, and his ethical exhortations to responsible freedom converge on life in Christ through the Spirit: "Through the Spirit, by faith, we eagerly wait for the hope of righteousness. For in Christ Jesus neither circumcision nor uncircumcision counts for anything; the only thing that counts is faith working through love" (5:5-6).

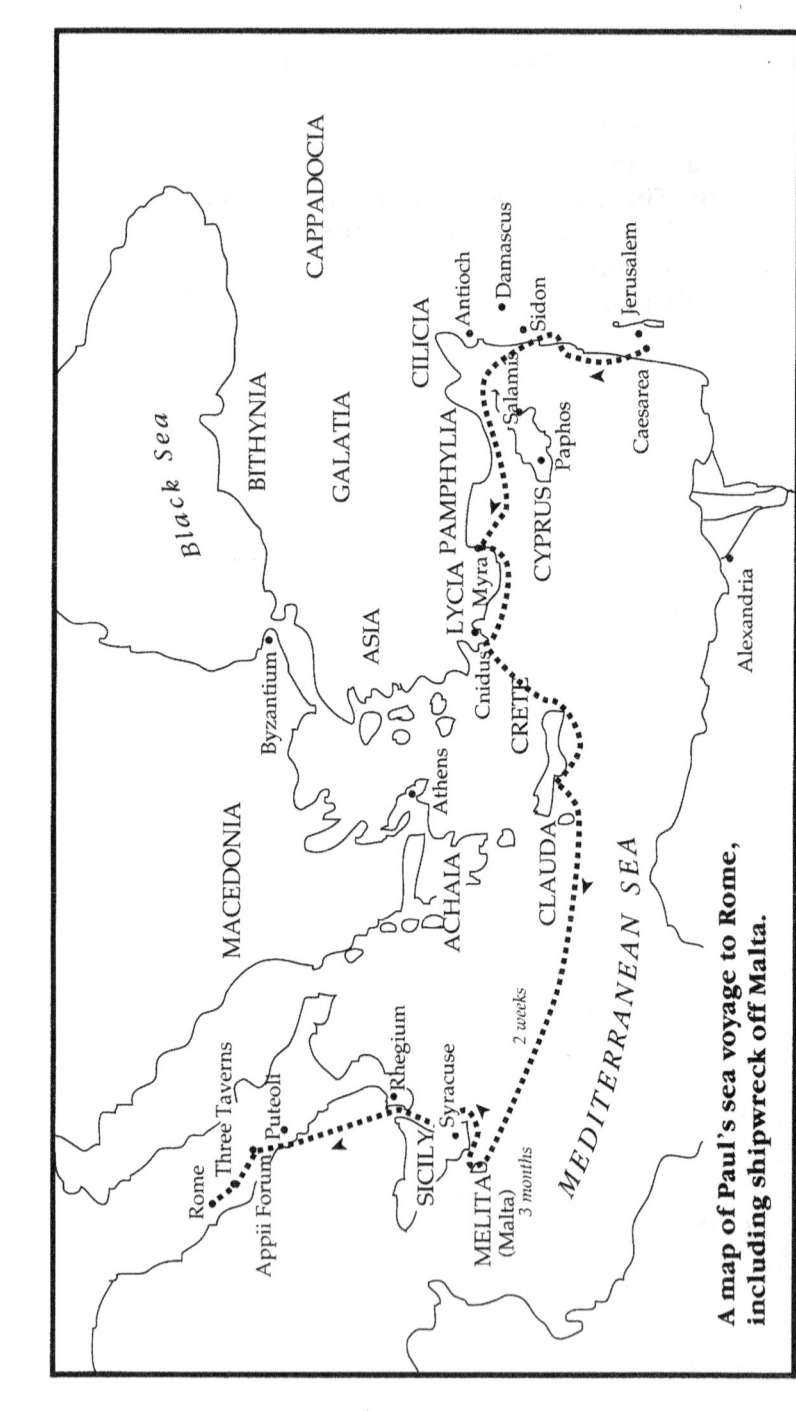

A map of Paul's sea voyage to Rome, including shipwreck off Malta.

Roman Christianity

Paul's letter to the Romans is considered his masterpiece. The letter has been given prominence by being placed first among Paul's writings in the New Testament. This letter is also unique among Paul's writings. First of all, it is addressed to a community which Paul did not found. Second, it does not have as its primary purpose the solution of particular problems which Paul had to address in crisis. Paul wrote to the Romans, probably from Corinth toward the end of his final visit to that city, in order to introduce himself to a Christian community which did not yet have direct contact with him. His major intention was to complete his missionary work in Greece and Asia Minor and to begin a new work in Spain:

> From Jerusalem and as far around as Illyricum I have fully proclaimed the good news of Christ.... But now, with no further place for me in these regions, I desire, as I have for many years, to come to you when I go to Spain. For I do hope to see you on my journey and to be sent on by you, once I have enjoyed your company for a little while (Rom 15:19, 23-24).

For this, he needed a new base with a strong Christian community, as Antioch had been for him in his previous travels. Rome would serve that purpose well, so Paul determined to prepare for his visit to that community by this letter of introduction.

Purposes of Romans

Paul felt that the best introduction he could offer of himself was his vision of the Christian life, thereby hoping to establish common ground with his Roman brothers and sisters. Thus, his letter is in large part a summary of what Paul considered essential to Christianity. Much of this vision he had developed piecemeal under pressure of the problems he had to fight in his various churches. Now he had time to draw many of these specific insights together into some general synthesis. We notice many themes that have already been treated in earlier writings, such as justification, attitudes toward Jewish law, the example of Abraham, life in the Spirit, and so forth, but now they are joined more closely to each other.

There are many scholars who think that Paul is doing more than simply giving this general overview of Christianity. They believe that he is also addressing a specific situation within the Roman church. This church was concerned about the relationship between Christians and Jews and about the implications for Christians of Gentile background, a problem not unfamiliar to the Pauline churches we have previously studied. We will get a better idea of how this situation took specific shape in Rome, if we look briefly at the historical and social background of that community.

Rome was, of course, a marvelous achievement of the ancient world. It began as a farming settlement, developed into a masterful military power, and gradually became the center of one of the most extensive empires the world has ever seen. It drew on the wealth, the produce, the art and the thought of its many lands. Its population grew to be huge and diverse, speaking many languages, expressing various cultures, and exhibiting a general openness to the pluralism of ideas and practices. Even today one can see the remains of the many temples, monuments, statues, arenas and other buildings which were witness to the power and the diversity of ancient Rome.

Among the peoples attracted to Rome were the Jews. They became a major force in Alexandria, Egypt, and in Babylon before reaching Rome, but we have evidence of Jews in Rome about two hundred years before Paul. By Paul's time there were about 40,000 to 50,000 Jews in the city. Because of Jewish support for Julius Caesar and then the support by Herod and the priestly families in Jerusalem for Augustus, the Roman emperors were generally favorable to the Jews. They permitted them to meet freely for worship and for common meals, allowed them their own courts, exempted them from military service and let them raise money for the support of the Temple in Jerusalem. Jews were among all the classes of society; even some members of the Roman aristocracy either supported them as so-called "God-fearers," or joined them as full converts. This is not to say that there was no anti-Semitism. While the Jews were accepted, they were not easily understood, and when they successfully influenced politics and the upper class, prejudice often reared its ugly head. The famous Roman orator, Cicero, offers an example in a trial speech disparaging the Jews as his way of defending a client who stole gold from Jewish merchants:

> You know how large a group they are, how unanimously they stick together, how influential they are in politics. I shall lower my voice and speak just loudly

enough for the jury to hear me; for there are plenty of people to stir up those Jews against me and against every good Roman (*Pro Flacco* 66).

It seems likely that the first Christians in Rome came out of these Jewish congregations. Because the Jews in Rome maintained contact with those in Jerusalem and frequently looked to this mother city for guidance, Jewish converts to Christianity probably came as missionaries from Jerusalem not long after Pentecost to found Christianity in Rome. This Christian minority would have lived among large Jewish communities, would not yet have been totally separated from the synagogue and, as far as the Romans were concerned, would have been indistinguishable from the Jews. A new phase developed as Christians increased in number and their teaching veered further away from Judaism. A dispute arose between the Jews and those among them who had become Christians. When their hostility threatened the peace, the Roman authorities intervened to suppress what they saw as an internal Jewish debate. The emperor Claudius forbade public meetings of these groups and expelled their leaders. You will recall that it was this expulsion that brought the converts Prisca and Aquila to Corinth during Paul's first visit there.

Certainly this early history made the Roman church sensitive to relationship with the Jews and raised the question of how many Jewish practices to bring into Christianity. The situation came into new focus by the time of Paul's letter, when the ban of Claudius was lifted after five or six years. By this time, Christians were meeting in their own household churches, Gentiles were entering the church in large numbers, and expelled Christians of Jewish background were returning to Rome to find things quite different from what they had left. There was a church, then, whose Gentile members were appreciative of Jewish Christianity and whose Jewish Christians were respectful of the Jewish community out of which they originated, but both were now functioning independently from the synagogues. This heightened their interest in how to relate with Judaism, a question that had been raised by the Roman church for some time before Paul.

Just how directly Paul was involved with this new situation depends on how one reads Romans 16, the final chapter of our present letter which sends personal greetings to an array of specific individuals. Scholars who think Paul is simply writing a general summary of the Christian message usually presume that chapter 16 was added to Romans and sent to Ephesus and other Pauline churches with greetings to many whom Paul knew in those other places. The assumption is that Paul would not have known so many people in Rome and was not directly concerned about the specific situation of the Roman church. He would, however, have known many in his own churches and would therefore have sent a copy of Romans to them with the addition of the special greetings of chapter 16. People included in that chapter are Aquila and Priscilla, whom we last saw in Ephesus after they had left Corinth. It is on such a basis that some propose Ephesus as the community that received a second copy of Romans.

Those who think Paul is more directly concerned with the Roman situation claim that his friends have returned or migrated to Rome, and that he is naming them in order indirectly to present people who might recommend Paul and his views to the Roman church. Among these friends would be Priscilla and Aquila, who are now said to have a house in Rome in which the Christians are able to meet apart from the synagogue. Confirming evidence lies in the fact that precisely when Paul is writing to his own churches he does not specifically greet many individuals because he knew too many or did not need to strengthen particular ties. In addition, there is weak textual evidence of a letter to the Romans with only fifteen chapters, and the customary concluding elements of a letter are found only in chapter 16.

Whichever is the case of Paul's intentions in Romans, he does devote chapters nine to eleven to the fate of Israel. He may have brought this up incidentally, because he was on his way to bring the collection for the poor to Jerusalem before travelling to Rome. It is likely, however, that his intention was bringing him to these chapters as the most important for the situation in Rome itself. What about the Jewish brothers and sisters who would not become Christian? Has God abandoned them? Paul's answers to these questions will reflect the sensitivity of the Roman church to its Jewish roots and will also reflect Paul's sensitivity to that situation of the Roman church. We will presume that Romans 9-11 are not simply a theoretical discussion after the doctrinal presentation of the preceding chapters of the letter, but that indeed Paul was preparing the way in the earlier chapters for a very pertinent point that would show his common ground with the Roman church. Before we look at Romans 9-11, however, we will outline the earlier teaching to see how it prepares for these later chapters and to see how Paul crafted his vision of Christianity for the particular context of the Roman church.

Paul's View of Christianity

The general synthesis begins first with what we might call the topic sentence of the entire letter in 1:16-17. We might paraphrase these verses as follows: "In the risen Christ God's saving justice is manifest, making just both Jew and Gentile who respond in faith." Thus, for Paul Christianity is not so much a doctrinal system, a moral code or a set of rituals, but a dynamic relationship between God in Christ and the human race. As Paul develops that thought, he begins with what we might call "the bad news," i.e., the condition of the world left on its own without Christ. He begins with a consideration of the Gentile world, a reflection not inappropriate for a church at the center of the empire. He says first of all that Gentiles could know God in the works of creation. Nevertheless, they find themselves in rebellion, turned in toward self and away from God, and filled with alienation: "They are without excuse; for though they knew God, they did not honor him as God or give thanks to him. . . . They exchanged the truth about God for a lie and worshiped and served the creature rather than the Creator. . . . They were filled with every kind of wickedness, evil, covetousness, and malice" (1:20, 25, 29).

Paul next points out that the Jews should not judge or feel superior to these Gentiles, since they, too, are in sin. Having the law as a gift from God, they nevertheless did not follow the law. Indeed, Paul observes at a later point in the letter, the law is not finally helpful, for it is manipulated by our sinful attitudes and we twist the law to our sinful purposes. The law arouses rebellion in us, suggests further evil we had not thought of, and imputes further guilt when we finally do not do what we should: "If it had not been for the law, I would not have known sin. . . . But sin, seizing an opportunity in the commandment, produced in me all kinds of covetousness" (7:7-8). This teaching about law is reminiscent of the same teaching in Galatians, but it is interesting to note the subtle changes in Paul's presentation because of the different situation in the Roman church.

In Galatia, Paul was addressing predominantly Gentiles and a group of Judaizers who were impugning his authority. He stated his principle of freedom from the law bluntly and without much nuance. Paul probably left behind him a great deal of misunderstanding which likely was aggravated by reports from the Galatian Judaizers to the Jerusalem church and which could easily have been passed on to the Roman church through messages from Jerusalem with which there were close ties. The Roman church was respectful of Jewish practices, so Paul had to clear up what he meant by freedom from the law if he was going to find common ground with these Christians. In Galatia, Paul was fighting the most reactionary of the four groups which we described earlier as evolving out of the debate between Antioch and Jerusalem. This group wanted to impose circumcision on all Christians. In refuting them, however, Paul may have left the impression that he opposed any Jewish law, not only for Gentiles, but even for Jewish Christians, thus seeming to be completely opposed to even the more moderate group represented by Peter and James. This would not have been pleasing to the Roman church, so Paul wrote with greater nuance to that church.

Basically, Paul still maintains freedom from the law, but balances his negative statements about the inadequacy of law with positive statements about its purposes and with sensitivity for those who wished still to observe it. Thus, whereas in Galatians 5:2, Paul said that Christ would be of no advantage to those Christians who were circumcised, in Romans 3:1-2, he mouths what was probably a question that the Roman church raised to such a claim:

"Then what advantage has the Jew? Or what is the value of circumcision?" He also gives a more positive answer, "Much in every way" (3:2), and goes on to show how the Jews have received the promises and that God remains faithful to these promises. Likewise, in Galatians 3, Paul stressed only the negative aspects of life under the law (it was a curse from which we needed rescue and a temporary guide until Christ came). Now in Romans 3:31, he answers what was probably another objection that the Roman community could raise: "Do we then overthrow the law by this faith? By no means! On the contrary, we uphold the law."

These thoughts will eventually lead Paul to considerations about the Jews in God's ongoing plan of salvation in chapters 9-11, but before we treat that section, we must finish Paul's description of the world without Christ and then the good news of how Christ finally saves the world. After Paul shows that both Gentile and Jew, with or without the law, are caught in sin, he points out the communal influence of sin, creating a climate of evil, and ultimately separating all from God. Paul calls this separation from God "death," and says that it enters the human race from the beginning as a communal effect of our complicity in sin: "Sin came into the world through [Adam] and death came through sin, and so death spread to all because all have sinned" (5:12).

The good news, however, is that God has not abandoned us to this fate. God's justice is a saving activity whereby God "justifies us," i.e., God strives to make us just and to reconcile us to himself and to one another. God does this by sending Jesus and raising him from the dead, giving us a share in Christ's life beginning with baptism, and pouring out the Spirit who makes us children of God, if we open ourselves in faith: "We are justified by faith, we have peace with God through our Lord Jesus Christ. . . .

God's love has been poured into our hearts through the Holy Spirit that has been given to us" (5:1, 5). Paul is also careful to say that while the Spirit does ultimately free us from the inadequacies of the law and gives us a better means of justification, the good purposes of the law are not thereby nullified: "God has done what the law, weakened by the flesh, could not do: by sending his own Son in the likeness of sinful flesh and to deal with sin, he condemned sin in the flesh, so that the just requirement of the law might be fulfilled in us, who walk not according to the flesh but according to the Spirit" (8:3-4).

The Fate of Israel

Having given this overview of what he considered the heart of the gospel, Paul then applied it in chapters 9-11 to what was no doubt an important question for the Roman church: What about the Jewish brothers and sisters who would not become Christian? Has God abandoned them? Paul gives a resounding "no" to this question: "Has God rejected his people? By no means! I myself am an Israelite. ... God has not rejected his people.... Through their stumbling salvation has come to the Gentiles, so as to make Israel jealous" (11:1-2, 11). In this statement Paul has given a view of God's working in history that makes room not only for the Gentiles, but for God's continued work among the people of the covenant of Israel.

The seeming rejection of Israel was only so that God might extend salvation to the Gentiles, but the faith of the Gentiles is to prod the Israelites to be themselves faithful to their covenant. God's saving justice is for all, and Paul insists that it is for Israel *first,* and *also* for the Gentiles. In these teachings Paul seems to tone down the harshness of his statements about Israel and the law, such as were in

Galatians and in other attacks against Judaizers. In doing so, he affirms the positive attitudes toward the Jews that would have been characteristic of the Roman Christians who came out of the Jewish community, but who also had to deal with their separation from the synagogue. In doing so, Paul also gave guidance to the Gentiles who now also comprised the Roman church, but saw their roots in Judaism.

Paul concluded his letter to the Romans with ethical exhortations that applied his general vision of Christianity and his teaching about the Jews. These exhortations appear in Romans 12-15: live as one body in Christ; love one another; do not fight or take scandal over the kinds of food one eats, or over which holy days one observes. There is room for Christians of both Jewish and Gentile background. In Romans 13:1-7 one ethical exhortation seems directed specifically to the Roman situation: "Let every person be subject to the governing authorities; for there is no authority except from God." Paul is not asserting absolute authority for civil government. It is always subject to God's law. But with that qualification, civil authority has legitimacy. Paul told these Christians that they could and should be good citizens in this center of ancient civilization.

He is writing at an early time in the reign of Nero, when the emperor was benevolent and there were hopeful prospects for the future. Thus, his view toward civil authority is more positive than negative. Nevertheless, even in this section Paul implies the criterion for judging such authority: "rulers are not a terror to good conduct, but to bad.... [a ruler] is God's servant for your good" (13:3-4). In other words, civil authority has legitimation from God when it serves to check evil and to serve good. When it promotes evil and impedes good, then it is no longer legitimate. Eventually, Paul will have to change his view toward Nero, but for this time he offers sage advice to his Roman community.

It seems likely that Paul succeeded in winning the esteem of the Roman church, for later writers indicate respect for both Peter and Paul as apostles of the church of Rome. Of course, Paul's arrival in Rome was not what he expected, and it is not likely that he ever reached Spain as he hoped. Paul travelled to Jerusalem after he wrote to the Romans and brought his collection to the church there. He was well-received by James and the moderate Jewish Christians (Acts 21:17-20), but received strenuous opposition from the Jews, perhaps at the instigation of the more reactionary circumcision party of the Jewish Christians. Eventually he was imprisoned, appealed to Caesar and was sent to Rome.

It is possible that he wrote from Rome his "letters from prison," Philippians and Philemon, though we have assumed that these were more probably written from an imprisonment in Ephesus. If he is the author, Paul would have written Colossians, Ephesians, 1 and 2 Timothy and Titus from Rome, but we have said that there is increasing doubt of his authorship as we move along that list. In any case, Paul was freed from prison when he reached the capital of the empire. "He lived there two whole years at his own expense and welcomed all who came to him, proclaiming the kingdom of God and teaching about the Lord Jesus Christ with all boldness and without hindrance" (Acts 28:30-31). The Acts of the Apostles end on that note, but reliable tradition finishes the story by telling of Paul's death close to the death of Peter, both in Rome under Nero's persecution.

Appendix:
Colossians and Ephesians

The letters to the Colossians and Ephesians are addressed as letters from Paul to these churches. The setting for both letters is purported to be Paul's imprisonment, and the prison has usually been taken to be the one in Rome, since Paul expresses no hope of seeing these churches again. Scholars, however, are leaning more and more toward the view that these letters come after Paul's time and do not reflect the same theology as in his other writings. They show familiarity with his style and message and build on it, but they also move beyond it. It is always possible, of course, that Paul himself evolved in his thoughts, and that is why scholars are uncertain about the authorship. There is more uncertainty about the letter to the Colossians than about the one to the Ephesians.

This latter seems less personal in tone and less concerned with the specific situation in Ephesus. It also copies from Colossians. Thus, scholars have proposed that Ephesians may be a circular letter expanding beyond Paul's theology for the churches of Asia Minor after Paul's time. Circulating this letter would have cultivated a suggestion and followed the example of the author of Colossians himself: "When this letter has been read among you,

have it read also in the church of the Laodiceans, and see that you read also the letter from Laodicea" (Col 4:16).

Both Colossians and Ephesians show churches that have grown both in vision and size. The Christians here seem beyond the earlier conflicts between converts of Jewish background and those of Gentile background, and they have moved beyond the earlier expectations of a near second coming of Jesus. They have also seen the church weather a number of serious difficulties. Now there are concerns about a larger institution, the development of its doctrine, and its need to organize for a long stay in history. Colossians and Ephesians develop further theology about Christ and about the church, and apply it to moral exhortations.

Unfortunately, we do not know much about the background of the church in Colossae nor about its particular problems. It is first mentioned in the fifth century B.C.E. by the historian, Herodotus, who called Colossae "an inhabited city, prosperous and large." It gradually developed as the most famous town in its region of Phrygia, probably because it had a good location along the Lycus river that flowed through the east-west valley in that southern area of Turkey, and because it was on the highway in that same valley that gave access to the interior of Asia Minor. The town was famous for its purple-red wool, called "colossinum."

By the time of Paul, Colossae may have been eclipsed by the cities of Laodicea and Hierapolis which were close by on the river. The letter to the Colossians indicates that Colossae had much contact and interchange with these other two cities in the valley. The letter also seems to show that Paul never actually visited these sites, but sent fellow-workers from Ephesus, such as Epaphras, Onesimus and Archippus. These three are all mentioned in the brief letter to Philemon and help us locate Philemon with his household church, also in Colossae. The letter to the Colossians may be linked a bit more closely than Ephesians to particular problems in that church, but it was written with a more general audience in mind, since its author intended the letter to be circulated. We do not know exactly what the problem was in Colossae, but it seems to be a false teaching combining Jewish elements with some sort of mystery religion. The author puts it this way:

> See to it that no one takes you captive through philosophy and empty deceit, according to human tradition, according to the elemental spirits of the universe, and not according to Christ. . . . Do not let anyone condemn you in matters of food and drink or of observing festivals, new moons, or sabbaths. . . . Do not let anyone disqualify you, insisting on self-abasement and worship of angels, dwelling on visions (2:8, 16, 18).

Apparently some people were insisting on worship of angels and other heavenly powers that stood as lesser deities between God and humanity, whether in addition to Christ or in competition with him. They combined this worship with Jewish customs, such as food regulation and feast days. There seem to have been other ascetical practices to humble and discipline the body, such as fasting or sexual restrictions, and somehow these were linked to cultic practices that sought trances and visions and a feeling of salvation not unlike those popular in the mystery religions. Finally, all these elements seem to have been interwoven as the secret religion of its practitioners, who alone had the knowledge that would enable them to be freed from this world below into the heavenly realm.

Whatever the problem, it led the author of Colossians to desire a more adequate Christology for his readers, and to develop a Christology beyond that of the previous letters of Paul. He establishes the sole authority of Christ over all powers, including angelic powers. He says that Christ has reconciled all things in himself, whether on earth or in the heavens, so that in him—and in no other power—we might begin to live in the heavenly realm. Indeed, in Christ alone is the fullness of divinity and there are no lesser deities between God and us or in competition with Christ. All of this contributes to what we call a cosmic Christology, declaring Christ Lord over all of creation. It also emphasizes a vertical relationship to Christ, rather than a horizontal one, i.e., it sees the eternal Christ in the heavenly realm as one who brings life from above to us below, rather than the historical Christ of the past who, as risen Lord, shares life with us in the present in order to transform us fully in the future. The author of Colossians sums this up beautifully in a hymn which he probably borrowed from early liturgies:

> He is the image of the invisible God, the firstborn of all creation; in him all things were created, for in him all things in heaven and on earth were created, things visible and invisible, whether thrones or dominations or rulers or powers—all things have been created through him and for him. He himself is before all things, and in him all things hold together. He is the head of the body, the church; he is the beginning, the firstborn from the dead, so that he might come to have first place in everything. For in him all the fullness of God was pleased to dwell, and through him God was pleased to reconcile to himself all things, whether on earth or in heaven, by making peace through the blood of his cross (1:15-20).

Besides this movement to a cosmic and a heavenly Christology, Colossians develops another description of the church, i.e., another ecclesiology. This is a theme picked up and more thoroughly elaborated in Ephesians, so we turn now to that writing. The letter seems not concerned with any specific situation in Ephesus, but it is of help briefly to consider the background of that church in order to appreciate why Ephesus might be the starting point for a circular letter with such a grandiose theology of the church.

During the New Testament era this city, with a population of about 250,000, was probably the fourth greatest center of the western world, after Rome, Alexandria and Antioch. Centrally located on the Aegean coast of Anatolia between Smyrna and Miletus, at the mouth of the Cayster River, this seaport city was a hub of commerce and culture for all of Turkey. Although it found rivals in the other cities on the coast, it nevertheless received primacy of honor twice as the Asian city to construct the temple to the reigning Roman emperor. It also possessed one of the seven ancient wonders of the world, the famous Temple of Artemis. Pilgrims came from all over to worship this earth goddess, originally a native Anatolian deity, but then a Greek goddess and also a Roman goddess under the name of Diana. She was associated with fertility and life, was chief protectress of Ephesus, and ruled over all cosmic powers. Both societal stability and salvation emanated from her worship.

Paul made Ephesus the center of his missionary work on what the Acts of the Apostles describes as his last missionary journey through Asia Minor and Greece. He wrote a number of letters from this city and stayed there for about two-and-a-half years. His stay was not without hardship, even to the extent of persecution and imprisonment.

Celsus' library of Ephesus.

Eventually he was forced to leave town. His preaching implied rejection of Artemis and of emperor worship. This was not only opposition to the established religion, but threatened political stability which the official public religion was designed to promote. It also had economic consequences, since the silversmiths felt a reduction in their sales of statues of Artemis. According to the Acts of the Apostles the merchants gathered in the theater at Ephesus, shouted Paul down when he attempted to defend himself, and forced him to flee to Macedonia.

While he suffered these setbacks, apparently he left behind a successful church. Again, according to the Acts, at the end of his last missionary journey, on the way to Jerusalem, he stopped at Miletus, summoned the leaders from Ephesus, and gave them a fond farewell with encouragement for their continued work: "Keep watch over yourselves and over all the flock, of which the Holy Spirit has made you overseers, to shepherd the church of God that he obtained with the blood of his own Son" (Acts 20:28).

We know from the book of Revelation that Ephesus was the center of Christianity in Asia Minor, the largest of the seven churches mentioned in that book. The city remained prominent into the next centuries. In 431, it hosted the Ecumenical Council of Ephesus which declared Mary to be the mother of God. It seems fitting, then, that Ephesus be the center from which circulated a letter with images of a universal, victorious church.

In the ecclesiology—or the theology of the church—in Ephesians several things are different from the letters of Paul. Paul's earlier image of the body of Christ focused simply on being members of Christ's body, i.e., on the diversity of Christians and yet their unity with Christ himself. Ephesians stresses more the distinction of Christ as head and the church as body, i.e., the corporate unity of the church as distinct from, though joined to, Christ as Lord. Also in contrast to Paul, this ecclesiology stresses the church as more than an earthly reality and as already experiencing in some ways the final heavenly glory communicated by Christ. In sum, whereas Paul speaks of church*es* of one place or another, Ephesians speaks of *the* church as a single universal reality already anticipating the final heavenly victory communicated by Christ its head or Lord: "[God] has put all things under his [Christ's] feet and has made him the head over all things for the church, which is his body, the fullness of him who fills all in all" (Eph 1:22-23).

Both Colossians and Ephesians draw specific moral teaching from their expanded Christology and ecclesiology. If Christ is cosmic Lord, then we must seek the things that are above. The only proper asceticism is love within his church and as his church toward the world. If his church is a corporate unity, then that unity must be lived in fact. This unity is to be expressed especially within the household. Recall that the household at that time involved more than the immediate family. It embraced workers and others dependent on the head of the household. For wealthier owners it would have included the slaves and freedpersons. They could all have had quarters in the house and would work on the estate or in the shop that might be attached to a residence. The early Christian communities were established out of these households, where often the entire group converted when the head of the house did, or where sometimes those who did convert had to get along with those who did not. Colossians and Ephesians formulate household codes of morality, exhorting especially the three main household groups to live in

Main street in Ephesus.

unity: husbands and wives, parents and children, masters and slaves. The codes do not eliminate the social structures, and presume male authority and the continuance of slavery, but they do call for mutual responsibility that will affect these structures and sow the seeds of eventual change.

Suggestions for Additional Reading

Barrett, Charles K. *Freedom and Obligation: A Study of the Epistle to the Galatians.* Westminster Press, 1985.

Brown, Raymond E. and Meier, John P. *Antioch and Rome: New Testament Cradles of Catholic Christianity.* Paulist Press, 1983.

Bruce, Frederick F. *Paul: Apostle of the Heart Set Free.* Eerdmans Publishing Company, 1977.

Fitzmyer, Joseph A. *Paul and His Theology: A Brief Sketch.* Prentice-Hall, 1989.

Grollenberg, Lucas. *Paul.* Westminster Press, 1978.

Johnson, Sherman E. *Paul the Apostle and His Cities.* Liturgical Press, 1987.

Malherbe, Abraham J. *Paul and the Thessalonians.* Fortress Press, 1987.

———. *Social Aspects of Early Christianity.* Fortress Press, 1983.

Meeks, Wayne A. *The First Urban Christians: The Social World of the Apostle Paul.* Yale University Press, 1983.

Murphy-O'Connor, Jerome. *St. Paul's Corinth: Texts and Archaeology.* Liturgical Press, 1983.

Stambaugh, John E. and Balch, David L. *The New Testament in Its Social Environment.* Westminster Press, 1986.

Theissen, Gerd. *The Social Setting of Pauline Christianity: Essays on Corinth.* Fortress Press, 1982.

www.ingramcontent.com/pod-product-compliance
Lightning Source LLC
Chambersburg PA
CBHW071451160426
43195CB00013B/2079